more free-for-the-eating wild foods

more free-for-the-eating wild foods

by Bradford Angier

Illustrated by
Arthur J. Anderson

STACKPOLE BOOKS

MORE FREE-FOR-THE-EATING WILD FOODS

Published by
STACKPOLE BOOKS
Cameron and Kelker Streets
Harrisburg, Pa. 17105

Standard Book Number 8117-1087-4
Library of Congress Catalog Card Number 69-16150
Printed in U.S.A.

DEDICATION

For my friend of many years and long one
of my favorite writers, Barbara Corcoran

OTHER BOOKS BY THE AUTHOR

BEING YOUR OWN WILDERNESS DOCTOR
(with E. Russel Kodet, M.D.)
THE GHOST OF SPIRIT RIVER
(with Jeanne Dixon)
SKILLS FOR TAMING THE WILDS
FREE FOR THE EATING
HOME IN YOUR PACK
MISTER RIFLEMAN
(with Colonel Townsend Whelen)
WE LIKE IT WILD
WILDERNESS COOKERY
HOW TO GO LIVE IN THE WOODS ON $10 A WEEK
ON YOUR OWN IN THE WILDERNESS
(with Colonel Townsend Whelen)
LIVING OFF THE COUNTRY
HOW TO BUILD YOUR HOME IN THE WOODS
AT HOME IN THE WOODS

CONTENTS

DIRECTORY OF WILD FOODS

WILD FOODS FOR SURVIVAL AND FEASTING

FROM THE FOREST AND WILDERNESS COME the tonics and barks which brace mankind," Henry Thoreau said more than a century ago. "There is a difference between eating and drinking for strength and mere gluttony. I derive more of my subsistence from the swamps which surround my native town than from the cultivated gardens in the village."

I didn't depend on nature that much when I was growing up in New England, not far from Thoreau's home, but wild foods I'd have the fun of gathering regularly enhanced our table at home. Too, I spent a few weekends with a couple of Boy Scout chums, camping beside a pond in a nearby forest and making it a game to dine exclusively on the wild fruits, vegetables, and fish the region furnished.

That interest in the free sustenance of the silent spaces continued when I moved to the high mountains of New Mexico and later to the Pacific Coast. It reached a peak, through necessity, when I was first struggling to support myself exclusively by writing in Alaska Highway country over a quarter of a century ago. In fact, the very first articles I sold—to

Sports Afield, Argosy, and other magazines—were on the subject of the edible wild plants that, along with wild meat and fish, were almost exclusively furnishing me with nourishment.

After later writing in passing about such wild fruits and vegetables in a number of books, notably *Living off the Country,* I made them in 1966 the exclusive subject of *Free for the Eating.* This considered 100 wild plants and 300 ways to use them. There have been those who have been interested enough in this volume to ask about other edible wild plants, among the many we've tried and tested, that have proved to be real gourmet delights. This book, then, is a practical, down-to-earth discussion of additional wild foods and a wide choice of delicious ways to prepare them.

Most of the recipes in this book are designed to provide servings for four people, but they can easily be adapted for different quantities. Another thing to keep in mind as you read many of these recipes is the advisability of using freshly ground black pepper when pepper is called for. It will make a considerable difference in the flavor of many wild foods, so you should have at the very least a small, inexpensive pepper mill.

Some of the best foods in the world are free. Long before we thought of raising them in our gardens and on our farms and ranches, all our commonest fruits and vegetables were growing wild.

Even today, in this age of space flight and split atoms, sustenance tasty enough to satisfy us in times of plenty and nourishing enough to keep us healthy if survival ever becomes a problem, grows free for the taking in yards, vacant lots, fields, along roadsides and seashores, on mesas, stream banks, lake edges, and within marshes and sequestered woodlands—

ready and waiting for those who recognize the bounties they hold.

What hobby can yield the same amount of pure and vigorous pleasure with so little outlay, and such delicious returns, as the gathering of wild foods? When you become interested in them, each excursion outdoors is transformed from a purposeless stroll to an eager, rewarding quest. Each trip becomes an opportunity for making new wild edible acquaintances and enjoying hours of stimulating exhilaration.

The kind of knowledge you will thus painlessly gain has saved more than one traveler from an untimely end. The truth is that innumerable individuals, if lost or stranded in the wilderness, would starve to death with ample food all around simply because they couldn't tell locoweed from wild lettuce. Yet for those who'll take the time to become acquainted with just the delicious wild edibles considered in this book and its companion volume, *Free for the Eating,* there will generally prove to be plenty of food at hand in any contingency.

"He may travel who can subsist on the wild fruits," Thoreau said, adding, "The cheapest way to travel, and the way to travel the furthest in the shortest distance, is to go afoot, carrying a dipper, a spoon, and a fishline, some Indian meal, some salt, and some sugar. I have traveled thus some hundreds of miles without taking any meal in a house and found it cheaper, and in many respects more profitable, than staying at home."

Outfitted with even less initial equipment, one can actually exist very comfortably—with ingenuity, perseverance, and a fundamental understanding of how to go about it. For example, wild turnips kept up John Colter's strength when that mountain man made his notable escape from the Indians. Sir John Franklin, Sir John Richardson, and other northern explorers lived for months almost entirely on the lichen known as rock tripe. In northern Europe and across the treeless top of Alaska and Canada, Iceland moss has kept actual thousands from starving.

"We are as much strangers in nature as we are aliens from God," wrote Thoreau's friend and neighbor, Emerson. "We do not know the uses of more than a few plants."

Yet all animals including man owe their existence to trees, leaves, stems, barks, roots, berries, grasses, aquatic plants, grains, and other forms of vegetation. In other words, plants are the immediate or ultimate source of all the world's food. Meat-devouring species are no exception to the rule, their dependence being at most a step or two away.

As might be expected, virtual thousands of such wild foods grace the meadows and forests, mountains and canyons, deserts, tundras, shores, and certainly the swamplands. "No one truly knows the outdoors," Ernest Thompson Seton pointed out, "until he can find with certainty a number of wild foods that furnish good food for man."

Adding from season to season the recognition of a few more can be, as you're perhaps already discovering, a practical and engrossing pastime, as well as a thrifty and healthful way of pleasantly introducing new delicacies to family and friends. Such acquired knowledge can even mean, in some unforeseen emergency, the difference between eating bountifully and starving. As the Royal Canadian Mounted Police says, "Survival is merely a question of knowing how to take advantage of the resources offered by the country."

It costs very little time, money, and effort to be ready for emergencies in which regular food supplies are not available. If you are not ready, it may cost your life. Besides, you'll be missing a lot of delectable dining along the way—and for free.

THE COMMON TREE YOU CAN EAT

PIÑON

(Pinus)

THE SOFT LITTLE NUTS FROM THE pinecones of millions of low-spreading conifers in the western United States and Mexico are not only pleasantly sweet by themselves, but they also afford prime flavoring for salads of the edible greens often seen flourishing nearby.

Roast the piñons first, after shelling them with the help of pliers or hammer, by spreading them in a single layer in a pan and placing it for 5 minutes in a moderate 350-degree oven. Shake the pan several times during the process.

Coarsely chop 1/2 cup of the toasted piñons. Mix these with 1/4 teaspoon each of grated lemon peel, tarragon, and salt, and with 1/8 teaspoon cinnamon. Shake well with 1/2 cup salad oil and 1/4 cup vinegar. This salad dressing can be stored, tightly covered, in the refrigerator. Use only about 1 1/2 teaspoons for every cup of greens. As exciting as a honking wedge of geese undulating across the blue evening sky, it will make everything taste new.

This unique salad dressing is just one of the reasons why the nut pines are valuable. The entire pine family, as a matter of fact, comprises one of the most vital groups of wild edibles in the world. The inner bark, eaten both raw and cooked, has saved hundreds of people from starvation. Aromatic tea, made by steeping the needles, preferably young, in hot water until the steaming liquid is well colored, contains the vital Vitamin C that both cures and prevents scurvy.

As a matter of fact, if you mistake a spruce, fir, balsam, hemlock, or one of the other coniferous members of the great pine family, you are still all right. These all furnish similar nourishment.

Specifically, the pines have needle-like leaves in clusters of from two to five which persist for two, three, or more years. The flowers appear in the spring, producing an abundance of yellow, sulphur-like pollen which enlivens the wind. Once this fertilizes the pistillate flowers, which are scattered among the new shoots, there develop the familiar cones which take two and occasionally three years to reach maturity and disperse their winged seeds on the breezes. It is only on the innumerable small, low-growing pines in the vast drier mountainous regions of the West that these seeds become large enough to bother with. They are regularly available in stores.

However, if the cones' seeds, no matter how greatly relished by squirrels, turn out to be small, at least there will be nothing unwholesome about them. Romanian cooks grind entire young pinecones and use them to flavor game sauces. Some Indians used to roast the soft centers of green cones by the fringes of their campfires and feast on the syrupy results.

The settlers early learned to gather the inner bark of the pines in the spring, dry it throughout the summer, and then grind it and mix it with regular flour. Next to devouring it raw, though, the easiest way to eat this sweet cambium is first to cut it into thin strips, then cook it like spaghetti. The bland flavor goes well with meat simmered at the same time.

Some of the tribes went to more elaborate preparations, even to making a sort of bread. The squaws mashed the cambium to a pulp in water, then molded this into big cakes. In the meantime, a rousing fire was kindled in a rock-lined hole. The coals were then removed, the cakes set in on green leaves, and the embers raked back over a thick layer of leaves on top. Damp moss covered everything, which was left to smolder for upwards of an hour. The cakes were then placed on pole frames and smoked for a week, after which they could be carried as trail rations. The results were so hard that before use the cake was customarily broken into bits and boiled until soft.

Even pine needles, when they are new and starchy, are pleasantly nutritious to chew on. Some Indians boiled the still firm, spikelike flower clusters, in which the petalless blossoms grow in circular rows on slender stalks, to flavor their meats.

The piñons have also long been important medicinally. Hot pine tea, made by steeping the needles or by boiling gum or pitch, was one of the earliest cold remedies. Chewing the gum was considered soothing to sore throats. Too, the resin was dried, powdered, and applied to sore throats by swabs.

The piñon resin was also used by various Indians, and later by white adventurers and settlers, as a cure for everything from rheumatism and flu to indigestion. Heated, it was applied as a poultice to draw out splinters and to bring boils to a head. This hot resin dressing was also smeared on cuts, burns, sores, abrasions, and insect bites. Applied liberally to a hot cloth, it was used like mustard plasters in treating pneumonia, neuralgia, and general muscular soreness and stiffness.

The pines as a whole hold a position near the peak in importance to wildlife, partly because many birds and mammals feast on the seeds and to some extent because of the year-around cover the trees afford game birds, fur bearers, and both large and small game animals. Grouse, pigeons, doves, quail, prairie chickens, and turkeys eat the needles as well as the seeds. Deer, elk, moose, and mountain sheep browse on the foliage.

If you've ever lived in New Mexico, you'll remember the fragrance of burning piñon enlivening the air, as it has been doing in this country for centuries. Thc piñon and its cousins, such as the Parry pine and the Digger pine, have long been the most important trees to the Indians in the Southwest. The women still use the nuts in all kinds of cooking, from soups to salads, and a pocketful of their almost airy evergreen flavor goes well at any time.

Incidentally, when you're foraging for piñons in high country, don't overlook the ungainly nests of the pack rat. Indians customarily break each of these rough, large retreats apart, often finding as much as several pints of nuts stored for winter use.

These rich little nuts found in the hearts of pinecones add a subtle sweetness to the already piquant flavor of young dandelions. To go with enough of these greens to serve four, get 3 tablespoons of salad oil sizzling in a frypan. Then stir in 1/2 cup of piñons, 1/2 cup of diced black olives, 1/4 cup seedless raisins, and a small mashed clove of garlic. After 3 minutes, put in the greens that have been torn to bite size, including a reasonable number of buds if possible. Reduce the heat, cover, and cook only until warm and tender. Season to taste with salt and, if you want, with a dusting of black pepper. Serve hot.

A delicious green sauce, flavorsome over steaming noodles or spaghetti, can be made with piñons and watercress. Start with 1/2 cup of chopped watercress, 1/4 cup piñons, a large chopped garlic clove, and 1/8 teaspoon of salt in the blender. When this is pureed, add 1/2 cup of freshly grated Parmesan

PIÑON

cheese. Conclude by slowly blending in 1/4 cup salad oil and 1/2 stick of butter or margarine. With fruit and perhaps a dry red wine, this makes a perfect meal.

When the Indians taught the early frontiersmen how to obtain nuts from the piñons and related low-spreading pines, they began an adventure in good eating that continues to this day. Piñon cakes are unique and delicious, both hot and cold. You can make them in camp, perhaps where you're gathering the nuts, or at home. In either event, the shelled nuts first must be chopped or crushed, as with a rolling pin, to a coarse meal. The easiest way to go about this, of course, is in the home blender.

If you're cooking over an open fire, just mix each cup of piñon meal with 1/4 teaspoon of salt and about 1/3 cup of lukewarm water to make a stiff batter. Get a tablespoon of shortening warming in a large, preferably heavy frypan until it is just short of smoking. Drop the batter from a tablespoon, flattening it into cakes with a spatula. Reduce the heat and tan the cakes slowly on one side before turning them to brown the other.

If you are at home, you can make a little less primitive cake by stirring each cup of piñon meal, then 1/4 cup of all-purpose flour, into a well-beaten egg. Drop on a greased baking tin with a teaspoon. Bake in a moderate 375-degree oven about 10 minutes until lightly browned. The flavor of these is even more delicate.

For about three dozen piñon bread sticks of unusual crunchiness and distinctive flavor, stir a package of yeast into a cup of lukewarm water. Once it has dissolved, pour into a mixing bowl. Add 1/4 cup olive oil, 1/4 cup salad oil, a tablespoon sugar, 1 1/2 teaspoons salt, a slightly beaten egg, and a cup of all-purpose flour. Beat until smooth.

Then add 3/4 cup piñons and enough additional flour, about 2 1/4 cups, to make a stiff dough. Using a floured board or square of plastic, knead this about 5 minutes until it is smooth and elastic, adding flour if necessary. Cover with a damp cloth and place in the refrigerator overnight or, if you are in a hurry, for at least 2 hours. In any event, plan your cooking so that the dough can later rise for another 2 hours, starting this recipe early in the afternoon if you plan to serve the hot bread sticks for dinner.

Divide the chilled dough into 3 parts. Cut each portion into a dozen equal slices. Using your palms, roll each piece into an 8-inch crayon-like strip. Place about 1/2 inch apart on greased baking sheets, brush with melted butter or margarine, and let rise until about double size. Salt lightly. Bake in a preheated moderate 325-degree oven for about a dozen minutes until crisp and barely golden. Either warm or cold, such crusty tidbits, their outdoorsy flavor becoming more evident with each bite, will really arouse the appetite.

Piñon crops vary in different years, but if you happen to run into a bountiful harvest, you may like to try some cookies. These are simply made in any desired quantity by mixing each cup of chopped piñons with a cup of brown sugar and the beaten white of an egg. Drop small blobs from a teaspoon onto a greased pan or cooky sheet. Bake in a slow 300-degree oven until lightly browned.

Or you can bake more elaborate cookies. In any event, piñon cookies will fill the house with a tantalizing aroma. Start the preparations for these by finely grinding 2 cups of blanched almonds. Lightly beat 2 egg whites. Mix these thoroughly with the almonds and with a cup of sifted confectioner's sugar. You may choose to omit this next step, but we now like to blend in 2 tablespoons of crème de cacao.

Shape the dough into cookies about 1 1/2 inches in diameter. Place apart on a well-greased cooky sheet. Brush the top of each with lightly beaten egg white. Arrange a half-dozen or so toasted piñons atop each cooky. Leave at room temperature all afternoon. Just before dinner, heat your oven to a moderate 350 degrees and cook the delicacies, which will number between 3 and 4 dozen, for about 10 minutes or until they are a light brown.

One of the most splendiferous edibles ever concocted by man is piñon torte. Beat 1/4 cup of sugar and a stick of melted butter or margarine into 2 egg yolks. Add 2 tablespoons milk and 3/4 cup toasted piñons. Mix together 1/2 cup all-purpose flour and 1/2 teaspoon salt, and fold that in. Whip 2 egg whites until they form short peaks. Gradually beat in 1/4 cup of sugar and fold that, too, into the batter.

Bake in 2 deep, well-greased, 8-inch layer cake pans in a slow 300-degree oven for 50 minutes. In the meantime whip a cup of heavy cream, sweetened to taste with sugar. Put the cooled layers together with half the whipped cream. Spoon the remaining whipped cream over the dome and garnish it with 1/4 cup of the toasted nuts, perhaps arranged in a pine tree pattern.

The flavor of chilled piñon soup is so satisfyingly piquant that this luxury is particularly refreshing on a hot fall evening. The soup is also excellent while still steaming. Because it is better appreciated when served in small portions, the following recipe will make enough for four.

Bring 2 cups of milk, a cup of game bird or chicken stock, a cup of raw piñons, a small diced onion, 1/8 teaspoon dried mint, and 1/8 teaspoon of black pepper, preferably freshly ground, to a simmer. Stirring occasionally, cook for half an hour over heat so low that only an occasional bubble dances to the surface. Then process in the blender until smooth. Either reheat for immediate use or refrigerate for serving cold. A palmful of minced chives scattered on just before bringing to the table helps bring out the savor.

A FAVORITE INDIAN FOOD TO EAT OR DRINK

CHIA

(Salvia)

WHEN CORTEZ AND HIS CONQUISTADORES advanced through the dry, open Southwest, they saw the Indians of that region using the tiny little brown, gray, and white seeds of the chia for food. A teaspoonful of these was regarded as sufficient to sustain an Indian for a day on a forced march. Too, when added to a cup of water and soaked for several minutes, the same teaspoon of chia seeds makes a nearly tasteless but extremely refreshing drink, especially valuable on the desert not only for its thirst-assuaging qualities but because it offsets to a certain degree the harshness of alkaline springs. Today chia is much more widely used in the back country of Mexico than in the United States.

You can go into some of the swankiest restaurants in interior Mexico and get a chia drink, either non-alcoholic or stronger. The basis for this is simply chia seeds soaked in cold water and used unstrained. A quarter-pound of chia to 1 1/2 quarts of water provides the usual proportion. The method is to mix these in a large jar or jug and allow them to stand for at least 5 minutes, long enough for the seeds to swell and to become opaquely surrounded with a gelatinous coating.

Then add lemon or lime juice and sugar to taste. This is usually chilled before serving.

This sage, a member of the mint family and one of the best known of all the Indian foods, thrives over much of California and northern Mexico. An annual that commences its growth when the winter rains start to sheet the plains and hills, it is nearly dead and rich with seeds by July. These, often beautifully mottled, are like the tiniest of slippery little flattened eggs.

The flowers themselves, blooming from March to May, grow in interrupted spikes of from one to four little, round, bright blue masses similar to others in the mint family. The projections of their outer parts are prickly. Below each of these heads arises a number of leafy bracts, often a bright wine color in contrast to the blueness of the blossoms.

The coarse, rough, deeply indented, dark green leaves occur mostly at the base of the small stiff plants, which are generally from six to eighteen inches high. Several pairs, however, decorate the stems, not enough to give the wind much purchase on these seed-heavy edibles.

The easiest way to gather chia is to take a large paper bag in one hand and a stick in the other, then to knock the seeds into the bag by striking the dessicated flower heads. Using large flat baskets, Indians used to do the same thing. Too, some of them cut and bundled the plants into the encampment. There they were laid on hard ground and the seeds threshed with rods. The women then winnowed out the seeds. In either event, they were cleaned and dried.

Some were ground into meal. This was turned into gruel or into hard, dark, highly nutritious cakes. The meal today is usually mixed in equal proportions with wheat flour or cornmeal, whereupon it adds a pleasantly nutty flavor to

A VERSATILE VEGETABLE, GOOD COOKED AND RAW

LIVE-FOREVER

(Sedum)

YOUNGSTERS OFTEN KNOW THIS WILD VEGETABLE as frog plant because of the way one of its fleshy green leaves, after being loosened by being held between the warm tongue and the roof of the mouth, can be blown up like a distended frog's throat. Our pioneer ancestors went one step farther and used the insides of the leaves, once they had been blown or cut apart, to apply to warts. The fresh leaves also have a cooling quality and have long been used to soothe bruises, insect stings, burns, and other such irritations.

The well-known live-forever, also called Aaron's rod, is a close cousin of roseroot, whose succulencies are discussed in *Free for the Eating*. As with roseroot, both the plant tops and the roots are deliciously edible, making them both pleasant table companions as well as prime survival foods.

The live-forever, which like roseroot is rich in sometimes life-saving amounts of Vitamin C, grows from Canada's Gaspé Peninsula to Wisconsin and as far south as Maryland. Good from early spring to late fall, it is a familiar of damp woods, moist fields, shaded roadways, and rich, stony banks.

The oblong, thickish leaves of the live-forever ascend stems one or two feet high in crowded spirals. Because of the way they can be inflated by blowing into the loosened slit at the base, they are unmistakable. Broad round clusters of tiny flowers, varying in color from crimson and garnet to whitish, appear in midsummer.

The stout, rounded or finger-like tuberous roots become stringy and tough when the plant blooms. Again in late fall, however, large masses of new-grown, crisp white tubers can again be located.

If you find them near home, you may enjoy making the following tasty relish from the roots, unless you prefer to wash and eat them raw as is or turn them into a sliced salad component. For the relish, concoct a pickle in the proportions of a cup of cider vinegar, a teaspoon salt, and 1 1/2 teaspoon apiece of cloves, allspice, and cumin. Bring to a boil. Then pour it over scrubbed young live-forever tubers that have been packed in hot, sterilized jars. Seal immediately, protect from drafts until cool, label, and store in a cool, dark place for at least a month before using.

Both the stems and leaves when very young are tender enough to enjoy raw. Later—until the plant flowers, in fact—they may be briefly cooked until tender by any of the methods suggested in this book for other greens. For a particularly appetizing topping for cooked live-forever, melt a stick of butter or margarine in a frypan. Add 1/2 cup of dry white bread crumbs and 1/4 teaspoon oregano. Heat until lightly tanned. Sprinkle this over the hot, freshly cooked vegetable.

The young tubers and greens together in the spring make a provocative salad. Rub a salad bowl with a halved clove of garlic. Then lay a bed of watercress in it. For each portion, spread on 1/2 cup of washed and sliced live-forever leaves and stems. Sprinkle over this 2 tablespoons of the coarsely chopped tubers.

If you are serving four, sprinkle 5 tablespoons of salad oil over the greens and toss. Mix 1/4 teaspoon salt and a scant

LIVE-FOREVER

pinch of dry mustard with 1 1/2 tablespoons of vinegar. Add that, grind pepper over the top, toss again, and apportion. If you are serving live-forever salads often and ever want a taste change, just sprinkle on a little paprika and freshly grated Parmesan cheese.

REFRESHING TONIC AND FLAVORING FROM THE FORESTS

WILD GINGER

(Asarum)

SOME OF THE INDIAN TRIBES REGULARLY used wild ginger roots for flavoring. This plant, one of the better-known wild flowers, grows in fertile woods from the Maritime Provinces to Manitoba, south to North Carolina and Kansas. A related species follows the coast ranges from British Columbia down into California.

Although the leaves are aromatic, emitting a pleasant fragrance when bruised or crushed, the roots are the part used and are milder than the unrelated ginger from the Orient. The plant is also known as Indian ginger, Canada snakeroot, and Vermont snakeroot—the latter two names resulting from the proclivity of the branching, easily gathered rootstalks to creep along the surface of the ground.

The beautiful long-stalked leaves of the wild ginger rise upon the rims of many a shaded stream, almost as if they enjoyed the gossiping of the brook as it gurgles past. These leaves, often heart-shaped and some three to seven inches broad, have sharp points and broad bases. Deep green above, lighter below, these are generally velvety with short hairs.

In the early spring a warm hue appears among the still undeveloped leaves. Presently a strange, dull bud—one to

WILD GINGER

every pair of leaves—protrudes its long tip from their midst. The flowers eventually bloom in May, often on short stems so close to the ground that the purplish red blossoms with their three long prongs are sometimes nearly invisible on the forest floor. These eventually develop seeds, nurturing them until they ripen.

There are two ways to use the roots of wild ginger, often gathered in early spring, after they have been well scrubbed. The first of these, common among the pioneers, is merely to dry them, grind them into a powder, and use them like the commercial spice they then resemble. Once regarded as efficacious in treating whooping cough, this is still commonly used in parts of eastern Canada as a remedy for flatulency. If you'd like to try it, just add 1/2 teaspoonful of the powdered or granulated root to a cup of boiling water. Drink this 2 tablespoons at a time as often as necessary.

Candied wild ginger comes close to being some woodsmen's favorite sweet. Wash the roots well and then cut them into short pieces. Simmer these until tender, barely covered with liquid made by dissolving 2 cups of sugar in each cup of water. Then drain, cooking the fluid longer if it still does not seem to be quite thick enough.

You can keep the wild ginger in the syrup, but many prefer to bottle both separately, first letting the pieces dry on waxed paper or foil for several days and then rolling them in granulated white sugar. This way you can use the syrup as a sauce for desserts, such as ice cream or sliced bananas, or you can mix a tablespoon with a cup of hot water and enjoy a steaming beverage that is both delicious and medicinal, especially after a heavy meal. The candied tidbits make wonderful nibbles. For a taste thrill, try some one day with a bit of cream cheese.

THE FRUIT THAT INSPIRES FAMILY PILGRIMAGES

WILD PLUM

(Prunus)

SOME FIFTEEN SPECIES OF WILD PLUMS abound throughout the United States and southern Canada, growing from Alaska and California to the Great Lakes and the eastern seaboard, where the fragrant white flowers of the prolific beach plum brighten the springtimes. They are close cousins botanically of the wild cherries, considered at length in my earlier book, *Free for the Eating.*

Wildlife does not use the plum so freely, however, foxes being the most avid diners. On the other hand, scattered thickets afford invaluable shelter for birds and small game. The fruit varies considerably, some of it being delicious straight off the twigs. The chief value of much of the rest is in incomparable jellies, jams, and other kitchen delights.

The beach plum, *Prunus maritime*, is a wild native plum which grows in abundance along the beaches, among the sand dunes, and on the coastal plains from Nova Scotia and New Brunswick to Virginia and inland, as around the Great Lakes. It is very abundant in Massachusetts, on Cape Cod and on the islands of Martha's Vineyard and Nantucket.

Growth and fruiting habits of the beach plum vary, a common trait in seedling plants. It resembles a bush more often than a tree. Some bushes sucker freely from the roots and produce dense thickets. The root systems are coarse, rangy, and deep, as necessitated by the usual bleak and dry habitat.

The fruit, which generally varies between one-half inch and one inch in diameter, varies in color from red through purple to blue and almost black. Yellow-fruited bushes are occasionally found. The natural home of the beach plum is in sandy, light soils or even the pure sand of wind-sculptured dunes. Most beach plums bloom profusely each year but sport a crop only once every three or four years. One reason for this is that they depend on cross-pollination. The weather, which is often very foggy or rainy, dark, cold, and windy during blooming, may greatly reduce or even stop insect flight so that there is no transfer of pollen among the self-sterile plants. Too, it may slow the growth of the pollen tubes so that fertilization fails.

Specifically, the beach plum is a sprawling shrub up to about six feet in height. It does not have thorns, although the oval leaves are sharp with sawtooth edges. The innumerable white flowers burst out before the leaves start to appear. The fruit, which occupies many thrifty families day after day and finds its way into stores, ripens during the sweltering weather of August and September.

Another wild plum that is often seen in country markets is the *Prunus americana*, a great favorite among the Indians, and a native from Montana to New England, south to New Mexico, Texas, and Florida. Its numerous branches, whose twigs are thornlike, have rough, thick barbs. The oval or oblong leaves, ending in long, tapering points, are sharply saw-toothed like those of the beach plum. The frail white blossoms, again appearing before the leaves in early spring-

BEACH PLUM

time, are extremely redolent. The red and sometimes yellow plums, appearing in late summer, are about seven-eighths of an inch in diameter, tough-skinned, pulpy, and usually sweet.

In northern California and southern Oregon many families make annual pilgrimages to wild plum orchards in and around the mountains and bring back luscious bushels of richly mottled yellow, red, and purple fruit, especially in the northern part of the range. Here the trees and shrubs are from three to ten feet tall, with ash-gray bark and occasionally spiny branches. The flowers, again appearing before the leaves from March to May, are white, fading to rose. By August and September, the branches are often loaded with the handsome fruit, its colors duplicated in the brilliant autumn foliage.

Here is a way to preserve wild plums that does away with the bitterish taste often found in such cooked fruit. Wash the plums and prick the skins with a sharp fork. Pack in hot, sterilized jars and cover with boiling water. Seal and process for 20 minutes in a boiling-water bath. Then cool, label, and store. When you open a jar, pour off the juice for jelly or punch. Pit the fruit and for each quart of plums mix a cup of sugar with a cup of cold water. Pour this over the plums and let stand half an hour. Then enjoy them whatever way your fancy of the moment dictates.

Such canned plums can be used during the winter to make some delectable rolls. For enough for four, you'll need a pint of the wild fruit. Drain the plums well, transferring the juice to a baking pan. Pit them and chop them into small segments. To the juice in the pan add 2 tablespoons sugar, a tablespoon of butter or margarine, and 1/4 teaspoon of powdered ginger. Bring to a boil.

In the meantime, sift together a cup of all-purpose flour, a tablespoon of sugar, 2 teaspoons of baking powder, and

1/4 teaspoon of salt. Cut 2 tablespoons of butter or margarine into the dry mixture. Beat an egg with 1/4 cup milk and 1/8 teaspoon almond extract and combine with the pastry to make a soft dough. Roll this 1/2-inch thick. Spread with the chopped wild plums, roll up, slice crosswise into 2-inch lengths, and place carefully in the hot syrup. Bake in a moderate 375-degree oven for about half an hour or until the rolls are done. Vanilla ice cream really touches up the individual servings, especially if you enjoy them hot.

The sharpness and tartness of wild plum compote make it ideal with game. For this recipe, pit a quart of fully ripe plums and cut them into small pieces. Grate the rind from 2 lemons and an orange. Squeeze the juice. Combine plums, rind, juice, 3 cups sugar, a cup of seeded raisins, and 1/2 cup good sherry. Bring to a bubble in a saucepan and, stirring frequently, simmer until thick. Spoon into hot sterilized jars and seal.

Along Cape Cod there are so many dozens of home stands selling wild plum jelly that many start to enjoy this at an early age. There are two secrets of making this delicacy successfully. First, pick the plums while they are still on the unripe side. Second, unless you have special equipment, make only small batches at a time, about three quarts at once being plenty.

Pick over and wash the plums. Barely cover them with water and bring this to a boil. Then drain, cover with boiling water, and cook about 10 minutes or until soft, mashing and stirring every few minutes. Squeeze either through a sieve or a jelly bag. Measure the juice and return to the kettle. Slowly add an equal volume of sugar, all the time stirring. Boil rapidly until 2 drops form on the edge of a metal spoon, then come together to run off in a sheet. This occurs at 220 to 222 degrees.

Pour to within 1/4 inch of the tops of hot sterilized glasses. Have paraffin melting over water, and tip a thin layer atop each nearly filled glass, turning and slightly tilting the container so that the edges will be sealed. Cool, add a second thin layer of wax, cool, cover with a lid or aluminum foil, and store in a dark, cool, dry place. This is excellent with game, lamb, poultry, and especially with rare roast beef.

You may also care to experiment by combining plum juice with other wild juices to make your own blend of wild jelly. A particularly successful combination can be achieved by mixing every 2/3 cup of wild plum juice with 1/3 cup of wild apple juice, then proceeding as above to prepare your jelly.

Wild plum jam is also good. Wash and pit a quart of ripe plums, keeping the fruit as intact as feasible. Put in a large saucepan, along with 1/2 cup of water, and bring to a bubble. Gradually mix in 4 cups of sugar, all the time stirring. Simmer for 15 minutes or until thick, stirring whenever necessary to prevent sticking. Remove the froth.

Spoon into hot, sterilized glasses. Seal immediately with paraffin. Cover to protect from drafts, which might break the glass, and leave to cool. Label and store in dry, cool darkness. Incidentally, any wild jams or jellies that are to be kept in a damp place, or mailed, should be put instead into vacuum-sealed or screw-topped jars.

Jam and tarts go together. To make enough of the latter for four, cream together a stick of butter or margarine and a 3-ounce package of cream cheese. Using 2 knives or a pastry blender, cut this into a cup of flour, 1/8 teaspoon salt, and a scant 1/8 teaspoon powdered ginger. Chill in the refrigerator. Then roll out in a thin sheet.

Cut into ovals with a glass, knife, or 3-inch cooky cutter. Place on a greased low pan or baking sheet. Bake in a hot 425-degree oven for 15 minutes. Then remove, make a concavity in the centers with the back of a spoon, place a spoonful of your plum jam in each hollow, dust with grated orange peel, and eat hot. These are rich but utterly delicious.

Wild plum pies are apt to be a bit on the tart side, and some like to combine the sliced and pitted fruit with an equal volume of peeled, sliced, and pitted peaches. Fill your uncooked pie shell with the fruit. Mix 1 1/2 cups sugar, 1/4 cup cornstarch, and 1/8 teaspoon salt and sprinkle over the fruit. Dust with a teaspoon of grated orange rind and dot with 2 tablespoons of chipped butter or margarine. Spread on a lattice top. Bake in a hot 425-degree oven for about an hour. Try this warm sometime with melting pecan ice cream.

Also sweet and odorous when served hot with ice cream, especially vanilla, is plum graham pudding. For enough for four, you'll need 2 cups of pitted, sliced plums. Mix 2 cups graham cracker crumbs, 1/2 cup sugar, 1/2 stick melted butter or margarine, 1/4 cup chopped walnuts, 1/4 cup cold water, 2 tablespoons grated orange rind, 1/2 teaspoon nutmeg, 1/2 teaspoon cinnamon, and 1/4 teaspoon allspice. Starting with the crumb mixture and ending with the fruit, place alternate layers into 4 small baking dishes. Bake in a moderate 350-degree oven for a half-hour, if possible arranging for the pudding to come out just when everyone is ready for dessert.

Wild plums, wild rice, and venison—all tasting the same now as they did when man first ventured on this continent—make a rugged, straightforward meal.

Let the venison come to room temperature before consigning it to a slow 300-degree oven for 12 minutes a pound.

Lay strips of beef fat over the roast. Baste it every 15 minutes after the first hour, employing a bulb-type baster. For the last half-hour of cooking, add a cup of washed whole plums and 1/2 cup of water.

When you've finally removed the meat to a hot platter and salted it, press what remains in the pan through a sieve to get a rich sauce which should then be seasoned to taste with salt and pepper and sweetened a bit with brown sugar if this last seems advisable. Bring to a simmer and serve over the sliced rare venison and steaming wild rice.

You can also use wild plums to mellow gin, a process favored by some of the colonists because it thriftily stretched available supplies of the ardent spirit. Wash 3 cups of wild plums, puncture each in a half-dozen places with a fork, and place them in a large jar with a closely fitting top. Add 3/4 cup of sugar and a quart of gin. Cover tightly and place in a cool, dark spot for two months, shaking the contents weekly.

At the end of that time, press the mixture through a sieve, return the sieved portion to the jar, cover again, and leave to clear. Then carefully pour or siphon the clear liquid in equal amounts into 2 quart bottles. Fill each nearly to the top with cooled water that has been boiled for 5 minutes if at sea level, and an additional minute for every extra 1,000 feet of elevation. Shake thoroughly, seal, and allow to mature for at least 5 weeks.

SPRINGTIME ON THE STOVE

COWSLIP

(Caltha)

THE GLOSSY YELLOW FLOWERS OF THE cowslip, also known as marsh marigold and by over two dozen other common names, are among the first to gleam in the spring along stream banks and in marshy coolnesses from Alaska to Newfoundland and as far south as Tennessee and South Carolina. This wild edible is also eagerly awaited in Europe.

One reason this member of the crowfoot family gained its name of cowslip is that you often see it growing in wet barnyards and meadows and in the trampled soggy ground where cattle drink. Few wild blossoms are more familiar or beautiful, and New Englanders find few wild greens that boil up so delicately so soon after the long, white winters.

The bright golden blossoms, which grow up to an inch and a half broad and which somewhat resemble large buttercups, have from five to nine petal-like divisions which do not last long, falling off and being replaced by clusters of seed-crammed pods. These flowers grow, singly and in groups, on slippery stems that lift hollowly among the leaves.

Cowslips, growing up to one and two feet tall, have crisp, shiny, heart-shaped lower leaves, some three to seven inches broad. These grow on long, fleshy stems. On the other hand, the upper leaves appear almost directly from the smooth stalks themselves. The leaf edges, sometimes wavy, frequently are divided into rounded segments.

There are two things to watch out for if you are going to enjoy the succulent cowslip. First, this plant must be served as a potherb, as the raw leaves contain the poison helleborin, which is destroyed by cooking. It is, therefore, a good idea to gather cowslips by themselves to avoid the mistake of mixing them with salad greens. Secondly, ordinary care must be taken not to include any of the easily differentiated poisonous hellebore or water hemlocks that sometimes grow in the same places.

The two poisonous plants are entirely different in appearance from the distinctive cowslip. The water hemlock plant superficially resembles the domestic carrot plant but has coarser leaves and a taller, thicker stem. The white hellebore, which can be mistaken for a loose-leaved cabbage, is a leafy plant which somewhat resembles skunk cabbage, one reason why that not altogether agreeable edible has been omitted from these pages.

The dark green leaves and thick, fleshy stems of the cowslip are at their tastiest before the plant flowers. The way many know them best is boiled for an hour in 2 changes of salted water, then lifted out in liberal forkfuls and topped with quickly spreading pads of butter.

For a change, you can cream them, too. Tear the cowslips into small pieces and boil for an hour in 2 changes of salted water. Then drain. In the meantime, be melting 3 tablespoons of butter or margarine, either in a saucepan over low heat or in the top of a double boiler. Stir in 3 tablespoons of flour and cook a minute. Then gradually add 1/2 cup of cream. Salt and pepper to taste, and stir until thickened. Add the cooked greens, mix well, and serve.

COWSLIP

Parmesan cheese also goes well with cowslips on occasion. Just use the above recipe, adding 3 tablespoons of grated cheese after the flour and other ingredients have started to thicken. Then stir until the Parmesan has melted and the sauce is creamy.

The leaves and stems aren't the only deliciously edible portions of this bright little harbinger of spring. You can make pickles from the buds, soaking them first for several hours in salted water, draining, and then simmering them in spiced vinegar, whereupon they take on the flavor of capers.

THE SHRUB THAT PROVIDES BOTH CAKE AND TEA

JUNIPER

(Juniperus)

BLACK BEAR, QUAIL, AND BAND-TAILED pigeon are among the game dining on the fruit of the juniper. These evergreen shrubs and shrubby trees with their compact branches, thin shreddy bark, and scalelike leaves pressed closely to the twigs grow from Alaska to Labrador, south as far as New Mexico and California. The usually sprawling evergreens prefer exposed dry slopes and rocky ridges, and many a hunter has lounged in them to glass the country or to watch a game trail. The not unpleasant sharpness of some of their short needles makes one feel warmer on a brisk day.

The fruit, whose flavor and aroma is familiar to anyone who has had contact with gin, is dark blue and has a bloom to it. Growing in large numbers on the shoots of the female shrubs, these berries are to be found the year around. They are the size of peas. The flesh surrounding the large seed is sweetish and resinously aromatic.

Indians used to dry and grind juniper berries and use them for cakes and for mush. The principal individual use today is as a nibble and as a woodsy seasoning. A few will take the edge off hunger. Too many, though, are irritating to the kidneys. In fact, a diuretic is made of the berries, a teaspoon of

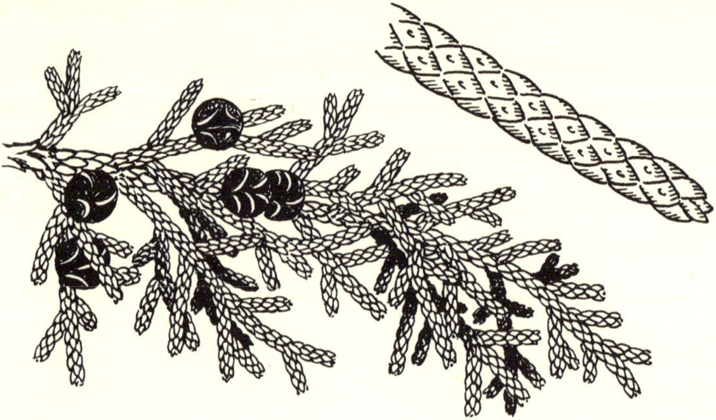

JUNIPER

them to a cup of boiling water, drunk cold, a large mouthful at a time, one or two cups a day.

Juniper tea, quaffed in small amounts, is one of the decidedly pleasant evergreen beverages. Add about a dozen young berryless sprigs to a quart of cold water. Bring this to a boil, cover, reduce the heat, and allow to simmer for 10 minutes. Then remove from the fire and steep for another 10 minutes. Strain and serve like regular tea.

THE ANCIENT AND DELICIOUS ANCESTOR OF A MODERN GREEN

PRICKLY LETTUCE

(Lactuca)

ONE OF THE MORE SUCCULENT MEMBERS of the wild lettuce family is the distinctive prickly lettuce, one of the ancient foods of Europe, from which it is an immigrant. Some botanists theorize that the lettuce we now buy in stores got its start from this species.

Like such Boy Scout familiars as rosinweed and prairie dock, the prickly lettuce indicates north and south, its sharply toothed and tipped leaves twisting edgewise to the sun. Both the lower part of the stem and the center leaf ribs bristle with prickles which, however, quickly lose their sharpness in boiling water. In fact, if you gather prickly lettuce young enough, it is tender enough for the most delicate of salads. Later, the leaf-clasped stalks of this wild lettuce grow up to about five feet tall.

When just a few inches high, it makes salads difficult to surpass. Wash enough of the tender young greens for four (four cups), shake gently dry, and keep in a cool placc while you complete the other preparations. For the dressing, blend 1/2 teaspoon celery salt, 1/2 teaspoon dry mustard, 1/4 teaspoon pepper, and a minced clove of garlic in a bowl. Stirring, add 1/4 cup of lemon juice slowly to the mixture. Stir in a teaspoon of finely chopped pickles. Then gradually mix in 3/4 cup salad oil.

Fry 8 slices of bacon until crisp, starting with a cold frypan and tilting it so that the grease accumulates to one side. Toss the greens with the dressing and with 2 tablespoons hot bacon fat. Garnish with the crumbled bits of bacon. Serve at once.

Or, still for 4 cups of loosely packed young greens, take 2 tablespoons of butter or margarine, 2 tablespoons flour, 1/2 cup sour cream, and 1/2 teaspoon of diced onion. Blend the butter or margarine and the flour over very low heat in a frypan, stirring constantly. Then turn up the heat slightly, add the sour cream and onion, and cook, still stirring, until everything thickens. You now have your choice. Either pour the sauce over the tender raw greens and toss. Or add the greens to the sauce and cook over low heat until they are limp. In either instance, season at once with salt and pepper to taste and serve immediately.

When the prickly lettuce is slightly older, in the late spring and early summer, here is a way to prepare it that is guaranteed to have the family eating with gusto. Stirring, sauté a teaspoon of finely grated onion in 3 tablespoons of butter or margarine until the bits are tender. Then add enough undrained young greens for four, scissored into bite sizes and then washed in cold water. Scatter on 1/8 teaspoon rosemary. Cook, covered, over high heat 3 or 4 minutes or until the lettuce is limp. Season to taste with salt and pepper. Serve hot.

Prickly lettuce also goes well in a casserole. To go with 2 cups of chopped or scissored prickly lettuce, heat in a frypan 3 tablespoons of salad oil and 3 tablespoons of butter or margarine. Add a finely minced small onion, a finely chopped garlic clove, and the leaves that have been washed in cold water but not drained. Cook over low heat for 5 minutes or

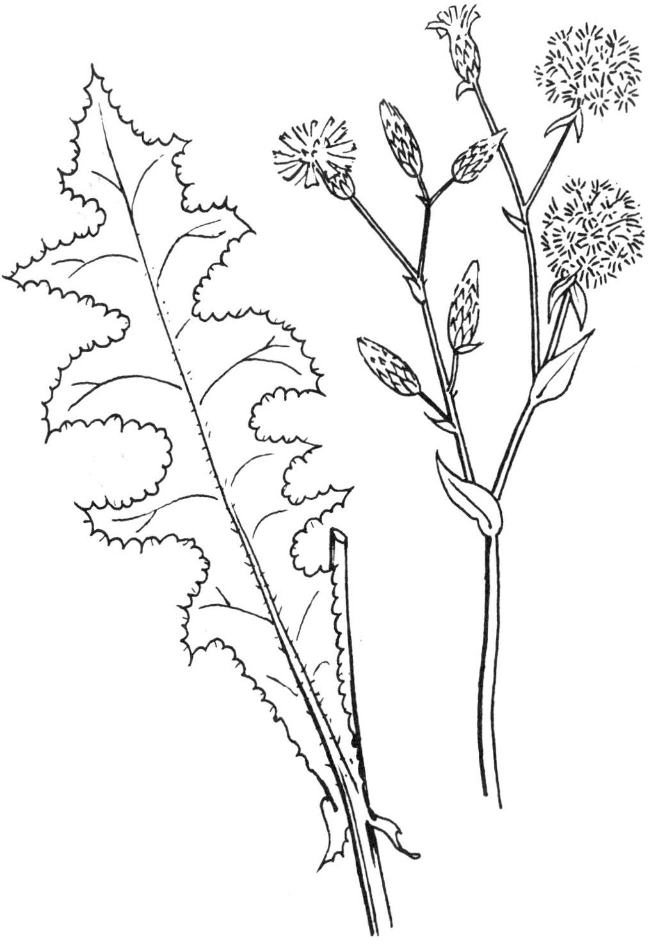

PRICKLY LETTUCE

until the lettuce is tender, salting and peppering it to taste. Then remove from the heat, allow to cool, and stir in 2 beaten egg yolks. Tip into a buttered casserole, dot with butter or margarine, strew with freshly grated Parmesan cheese, and brown in an oven preheated to a moderate 400 degrees.

A vinegar and bacon sauce brings out the singular taste of prickly lettuce in the following dish. To go with 2 cups of cooked greens, sauté a small diced onion and 2 tablespoons of diced green pepper in 1/4 cup of bacon drippings. When they are soft, add 1/4 cup lemon juice, 1/2 teaspoon salt, and 1/8 teaspoon pepper. Allow to bubble several minutes. Then add the well-drained lettuce and heat well. Serve steaming, garnished with mealy slices of hard-cooked eggs that have been touched up with paprika and the merest suggestion of oregano.

You can top off the prickly lettuce season by bringing 2 tablespoons each of salad oil and butter or margarine, along with the two halves of a clove of garlic, to a sizzle in the bottom of a saucepan. Add enough washed, undrained greens for four. Stir until they start to go limp. Then cover and cook until thoroughly tender. Take out the garlic. Puree what's left in the blender or press through a sieve.

Return to the saucepan. Season to taste with pepper and salt. Stir in 1/2 teaspoon lemon juice. Then add a cup of rich milk, bring slowly to a simmer, and serve on hot buttered toast with a sliced hard-cooked egg garnishing each portion.

A NUTRITIONAL ADDITIVE FOR SOUPS AND STEWS

ROCK TRIPE

(Umbilicaria)

PROBABLY THE MOST WIDELY KNOWN OF the wild foods of the Far North is the lichen called rock tripe, whose growth reaches into the southern states. Rock tripe resembles a leathery dark lettuce leaf, up to some three inches across, attached at its center to a rocky surface. Unless the day is wet, rock tripe is apt to be rather dry. It can be eaten raw,

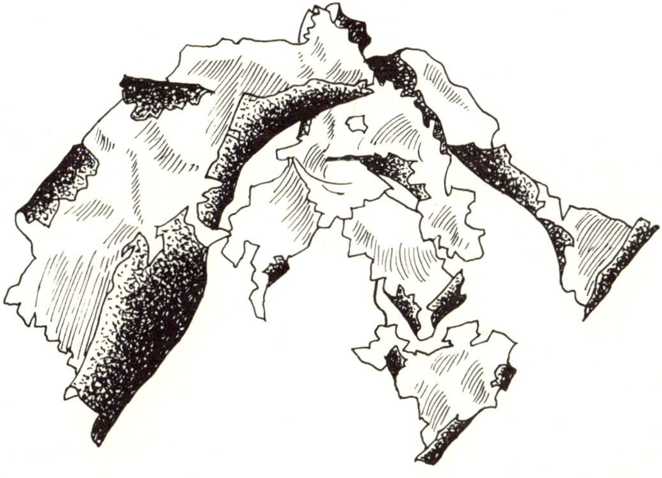

ROCK TRIPE

especially in small amounts, but you'll probably prefer it much of the time boiled to thicken soups and stews.

Rock tripe is one of the lichens that manufacture soil by disintegrating rock, so it is apt to be rather gritty. Wash it as well as possible, preferably soaking it in water for several hours to rid it of its purgative, bitter character. The flavor will then be improved if you roast it in a pan, before the campfire or in a partially open oven, until it is dry and crisp.

Then simmer it slowly for an hour or so, or until tender, whereupon it will impart a gumbo-like thickness to the stew or soup. Depending on the main ingredients, this may be short on taste, but it will be surpassingly long on nourishment.

This lichen was widely used as an emergency food in early trapping and Arctic-exploring days. Franklin, Richardson, and other northern adventurers lived on rock tripe for months with hardly any change of diet.

STILL ABUNDANT FRUIT OF INDIANS AND PIONEERS

GRAPE

(Vitis)

THE VARIOUS SPECIES OF BROAD-LEAVED, tendril-clinging, high-climbing or trailing wild grapes, one of the survival foods of the Lewis and Clark expedition and long an Indian mainstay throughout much of the continent, include the large fox grape, the aromatic muscadine, the pleasant pigeon grape, and the notable scuppernong. All are too familiar to require description.

At least half the world's wild grapes are native to this country, some two dozen or so species being widely distributed over the United States. Favoring moist, fertile ground, they frequently twine towards sunlight along stream banks, beaches, fences, stone walls, and near the edges of woods. Birds find the dense foliage excellent sanctuary and even use the bark for some of their nests.

Fruit, leaves, and young shoots are all edible. Among the game making use of them are deer, black bear, opossum, rabbit, squirrel, dove, wood duck, ruffed grouse, ring-necked pheasant, bobwhite, prairie chicken, and wild turkey. Even when clusters of fruit dry like raisins on the vines, they are sought by birds and animals during off seasons.

There are two satisfactory ways of securing wild grape juice for use in the home. For the first, wash, pick over, and stem your grapes. Have hot, sterilized quart jars waiting, arranged on toweling out of drafts, and have water boiling. Tip 2 cupfuls of wild grapes into each jar. Add a cup of sugar to each, planning to sweeten it more later if necessary. Fill with boiling water. Seal immediately, allow to cool, label, and then store in a dark, cool place for about 10 weeks before straining and using.

For the second, again wash, pick over, and stem your wild fruit. Mash the grapes in a kettle, not crushing the seeds. Cover with a minimum of water and bring to a simmer only. Heat that way for a half-hour, with only an occasional bubble plopping to the top. Press through a sieve and then strain through a jelly bag. Season to taste with white sugar. Bring once more to a simmer, not a boil, for 15 minutes. Pour into hot, sterilized jars set on a towel, seal, cool as always away from drafts that might break the glass, label, and store in a dark, cool, dry place.

For a sherbet with a satisfying bouquet, mix and chill in ice trays—with the refrigerator control set for fast freezing—2 cups of wild grape juice, 3 cups milk, 1/4 cup crushed pineapple, a tablespoon lemon juice, and sugar to taste. This is even better when you use half-and-half instead of the whole milk. Freeze until nearly firm. Then turn into a chilled bowl and beat, with either a rotary hand or electric beater, until smoothly blended. Turn back into the trays and freeze, stirring once or twice, until almost firm.

Wild grape jelly is luscious, but it takes some doing. The majority of the grapes should be on the underripe side. Wash, drain, and stem these. Relegate them to a kettle, mash them without crushing the seeds, and simmer until the fruit comes apart. Press through a sieve and then, not exerting any pressure, allow to drip through a jelly bag.

When the time comes to make the jelly, prepare only a

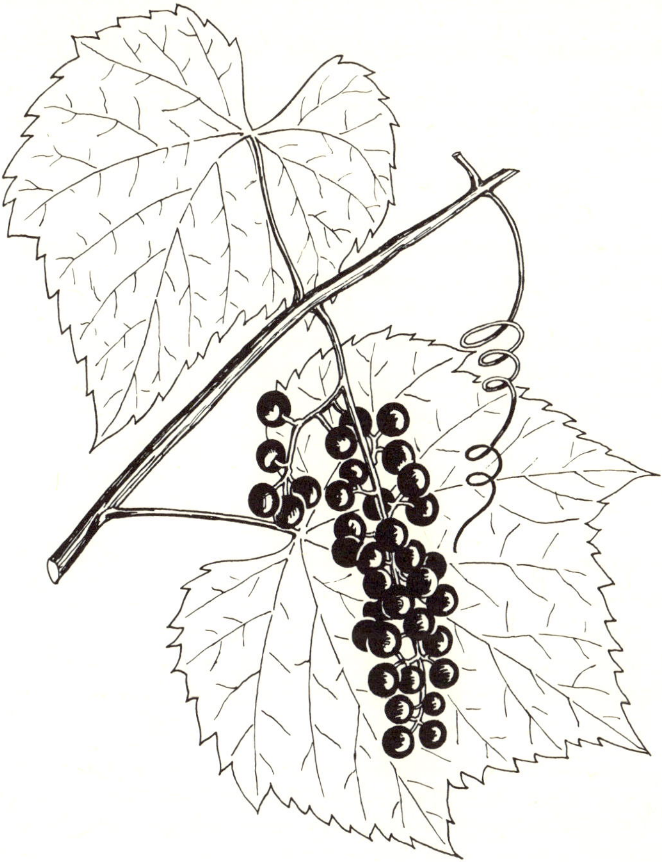

GRAPE

quart of this juice at a time for perfect jelly. Here's another secret, too. Ordinary grape jelly has a tendency to crystallize upon standing. An easy way to prevent this? When preparing the juice, just cook a cup of diced tart apples with each 4 cups of wild grapes.

Allow 4 cups of sugar to every 4 cups of juice. Bring rapidly to a boil. Continue boiling until 2 drops form on the edge of a metal spoon, then flow together to make a sheet. The jelling point will near at 220 to 222 degrees if you're using the thermometer. Skim off the foam. Then pour the sweetened juice into hot, sterilized glasses, filling these to within 1/4 inch of the top.

Either vacuum seal, if you are using that kind of a container, or seal with paraffin, melting this in small bits over hot water and pouring a thin layer atop the jelly, carefully turning and tipping the glass so that the seal is perfect. Allow to cool. Then pour on a second thin layer of paraffin, cool, cover with a lid or with foil, label, and store in a cool, dark sanctuary.

Some may recall their grandmothers making wild grape conserve. They may even remember being allowed to help her, until their interest waned, for the pleasure of squeezing the individual wild grapes—which perhaps grew luxuriously on the edge of the apple orchard—until the insides plopped out of their skins.

The pulp goes into one pan, the skins along with a cup of water for every 4 pounds of washed and stemmed grapes in another. Both are simmered over low heat for 15 minutes, until the skins cook down and the seeds become dislodged from the pulp. Then press the pulp through a sieve to remove the seeds. You'll have a smoother conserve if you now take time to chop the skins, along with the cup of seedless raisins that go in next. Also chop a navel orange, plus a segment of skin about the size of a silver dollar.

Combine all this in a single pan, stir in 4 cups of sugar and 1/2 teaspoon of salt, and simmer over moderate heat for half an hour, stirring frequently and spooning off any foam. When everything has thickened, you can give it a little added substance by stirring in a cup of finely chopped nutmeats. Many in the East use hazelnuts but if you're away from where they thrive, try substituting a cup of slivered almonds. Pour the thick mixture into small, hot, sterilized jars, seal immediately, and treat as usual. You owe it to yourself to try this with venison or savory beef.

Pie, anyone? Squeeze the skins from 4 cups of ripe wild grapes. Simmer the pulp until it comes apart and press it through a sieve to remove the seeds. Chop the skins into fine bits. Now blend the strained pulp and the chopped skins with 1 1/2 cups sugar, 2 tablespoons flour, a well-beaten egg, a tablespoon of lemon juice, and 1/4 teaspoon salt.

Turn into an uncooked 9-inch pie shell, dot with 2 tablespoons of chipped butter or margarine, tightly fit on a top crust, and cut a pine tree of slits in the center. Bake in a preheated hot 450-degree oven for 10 minutes. Then lower the heat to a moderate 350 degrees and bake 20 minutes longer or until the crust is attractively bronzed.

Unless you have your own favorite pastry recipe, here is a good one for wild grape pie. Cut 2/3 of a cup of shortening into 2 cups of sifted all-purpose flour and a teaspoon salt until you have particles the size of peas. Stir in about 1/3 cup of cold water, a bit at a time, enough to make a wad of dough. Divide this into 2 parts and lightly roll out about 1/8-inch thick.

If you, too, enjoy dining occasionally at Middle East restaurants, you are already acquainted with the delicate acid savor grape leaves lend to food. To use them for cooking, these should be gathered in the spring when they have achieved their growth but are still tender.

A convenient way to keep several dozen for future use is to divide such freshly gathered leaves into piles of 2 dozen each. Fold each of these stacks once and tie it together with a string. Bring a large pot of water to a boil and add salt until no more will dissolve—about 3/4 cup of salt to 3 quarts of water. Then dip each bundle into the boiling brine for 5 seconds.

Press the stacks tightly into sterilized jars, tip in a bit of the saturated salt solution to condense and keep the leaves from becoming too brittle. Store in a dark, cool, dry place. These can be used—as long as they last—until the following spring, by which time you'll have a new crop of raw material. Before employing any of them, incidentally, always wash the leaves well in cold fresh water.

Stuffed grape leaves, far simpler to prepare than they may sound, are as exciting as they are exotic. Mix 1 1/2 pounds ground lean beef, venison, lamb, or veal with 3/4 cup of raw rice, 2 raw eggs, a small grated onion, 1/4 cup minced celery, 1/8 teaspoon apiece of marjoram and thyme, and salt and pepper to taste. Place about a tablespoon of this mixture on each grape leaf, well washed if they have been salted down, and wrap each neatly around it.

Sauté 4 diced slices of bacon in the bottom of a large kettle until they start to tan. Pour in 3 cups of canned tomatoes and bring to a simmer. Now carefully spoon the stuffed grape leaves into the hot mixture, top with another 3 cups of canned tomatoes, cover, and cook over moderate heat for an hour with only an occasional bubble ballooning to the top. Serve hot.

Such game birds as grouse take on added zest when cooked with grape leaves. Rub each cleaned and plucked small fowl inside and out with lemon juice, salt, and a sprinkling of powdered ginger and black pepper. Lard generously with thin strips of salt pork.

Place atop a nest of grape leaves in a shallow baking dish. Cover with additional leaves. Roast 30 to 40 minutes in a slow 300-degree oven until a sharp fork can be easily inserted and withdrawn. Remove the top leaves and the lardons. Then turn the heat up to a hot 500 degrees just long enough to give the birds an appetizing bronze. Sprinkle with white bread crumbs, browned in an abundance of butter or margarine, and clear a way to the table.

RICH AND NEARLY INEXHAUSTIBLE DELICACY FROM THE SEA

IRISH MOSS

(Chondrus)

SCIENTISTS ARE FINDING A RICH AND nearly inexhaustible store of foods in the oceans that cover almost three-fourths of the globe's surface. Not the least of these is Irish moss, familiar on the eastern shores of this continent as well as in Europe, where it has been eaten for centuries.

Replete in such valuable elements as sodium, potassium, magnesium, copper, calcium, phosphorus, chlorine, and sulphur, this starchy seaweed is also an excellent source of iodine. Furthermore, it is so digestible that it is recommended for convalescents. As if all that weren't enough, it is good the year around.

Also known as sea moss, pearl moss, and carrageen moss, this marine alga was widely gathered and kept for years by our forefathers who settled along the Atlantic Coast. Clinging to submerged rocks, it is gathered during low tides. Irish moss that has been cast up along the shore by tides can also be harvested, often already bleached by the sun. Commercial processors bleach their product in the sunlight to a creamy white. However, the natural, dark Irish moss has even more vitamins.

Irish moss is naturally greenish, purplish, reddish, brown,

IRISH MOSS

and blackish. Attached to submerged rocks by small disks, it consists of flat, cartilaginous, forked stems or fronds up to about a foot long. Although it has a rather pleasant mucilaginous, saline taste, it is too tough to eat raw. Drying it makes it almost bonelike.

But just a small amount of cooking after it has been well washed in fresh water will tenderize it, and it can be eaten in a number of ways. It is just the extract that is commonly used. However, a handful cut up and cooked with a soup or stew makes a tasty and thickening additive. Soup made from Irish moss and fresh water alone, or the jelly that it forms upon cooling, is a palatable and nourishing emergency food.

Irish moss, as well as being nutritious, is also soothing to the digestive tract, and it used to be considered useful in allaying diarrhea. The dose was a teaspoon of the dried plant in a cup of boiling water, drunk cold one or two cupfuls a day, several sips at a time.

Irish moss lemonade used to be recommended for anyone who was suffering from a cold or otherwise indisposed. To make a quart of this, start by soaking 1/2 cup of the moss until soft in enough cold water to cover. Then drain, add the moss and a quart of boiling water to the top of a double boiler, and simmer about half an hour until the moss is dissolved. Strain, add the juice of 2 fresh lemons, sweeten to taste, and share with your patient.

Blancmange can be a treat for both invalid and gourmet. Properly, you'll need the bleached variety for this. Wash the moss well to remove any sand and pick out any discolored pieces. Add the remainder to a quart of milk in the top of a double boiler and cook half an hour. Then strain. Flavor to taste with salt, sugar, and one of the extracts such as vanilla. Pour into molds that have been immersed in cold water. Set aside, perhaps in the refrigerator, to become firm. Many like this with cream and sliced, sugared oranges. Another tasty variation is a chocolate sauce with overtones of peppermint extract.

If you like meat jelly, there's an easy way to have it with Irish moss. Just wash 1/2 cup of the moss in fresh water. Add it to a quart of broth and let stand half an hour. Then bring it to a simmer, preferably in the top of a double boiler. Stirring, cook it for 10 minutes. Then strain and, if you want, pour into molds.

Irish moss salad is different as well as delicious. Start by washing some of the picked-over seaweed in hot water, then placing it in a soup plate, and covering it with the heated juice of 3 lemons. After several hours the moss will have dissolved, hardening everything into a yellow jelly. Place this in the refrigerator to chill and become even firmer. If you start all this in the early afternoon, it will be ready by dinnertime.

Then arrange a few cool, crisp lettuce leaves on each of four chilled salad plates. Cut the moss mixture into sparkling golden cubes and center them on the lettuce. Cut into small cubes 2 cups of the tastiest apples you can come by. Mix these with 1 1/4 cups of finely diced celery and 3 tablespoons mayonnaise. Distribute this among the individual salads and top each with a few walnuts. This is so good it's almost voluptuous.

WILD COUSIN OF THE DOMESTIC APPLE

HAWTHORN

(Crataegus)

IT IS FORTUNATE THAT IT'S EASY to distinguish the hawthorn from other shrubs and small trees. Even the professionals find it difficult to identify the separate species, the number of which in the United States is estimated to run all the way from about 100 to as high as 1,200. They grow from one coast to the other, making them valuable when survival is a problem. Taste varies considerably, and the only way to determine the edibility of hawthorn you've come across is by sampling. The better of them are delicious raw and when turned into jelly require very little sugar.

These cousins of the domestic apple are also known as thorn apples, thorn plums, thorns, mayhaws, red haws, scarlet haws, haws, cockspur thorn, etc. Wood ducks eat the fruit. Pheasants, grouse, pigeons, and turkeys relish both buds and fruit. Black bears, rabbits, beavers, raccoons, and squirrels include both fruit and bark in their diets. Deer browse on the foliage and the apple-like pomes. In addition to all this, hawthorns provide almost impregnable nesting places.

You can readily identify a hawthorn even in winter, particularly as the long, sharp, usually straight, occasionally slightly curved thorns, ranging in length up to about five inches, are not shared by any of our other native trees and shrubs.

HAWTHORN

Showy when blossoming in the spring and attractive when colorful with fruit, especially against the snow, hawthorns thrive in sunny locales in clearings, pastures, abandoned fields, and along roads and fences. The white and occasionally pinkish flowers, which have five petals, grow in terminal clusters. The fruit, which is usually red but sometimes greenish or yellowish, looks like tiny apples. Each contains one to five bony, one-seeded nutlets.

The part of the fruit that isn't seed is somewhat dry, and you'll need a lot of it, but the jelly made from hawthorns is golden and intriguing. Cover the berries with water and simmer them until they are soft, stirring them occasionally to prevent their sticking. Add more hot water if they start to run dry. Then put the results in a jelly bag, squeezing this to get out the last drop of juice. Depending on the particular fruit, it will take about 2 pounds of the berries to make the following recipe.

Stir a package of pectin into 4 cups of the juice. Continuing to stir, bring to a boil over high heat. Add 6 cups of sugar and stirring, bring to a full rolling boil for 2 minutes. Then remove from the heat, skim off the foam, and pour to within 1/4 inch of the tops of hot, sterilized jelly glasses that are standing on a towel away from drafts. Seal with a thin layer of melted paraffin, carefully tilting each of the glasses so that this will adhere evenly to the sides. When it has cooled, add a second coating. Cool gradually, cover with regular caps or with aluminum foil, label, and store in a cool, dry place.

THE CHOICE NUTRIMENT THAT EGYPTIANS PUT IN THEIR TOMBS

CHUFA

(Cyperus)

CHUFA WAS SO VALUED AS A nutriment during early centuries that as long as 4,000 years ago the Egyptians were including it among the choice foods placed in their tombs. Wildlife was enjoying it long before that. Both the edible tubers of this plant, also known as earth almond and as nut grass, and the seeds are sought by waterfowl, upland game birds, and other wildlife. Often abundant in mud flats that glisten with water in the late fall and early winter, the nutritious tubers are readily accessible to duck. Where chufa occurs as a robust weed in other places, especially in sandy soil and loam, upland game birds and rodents are seen vigorously digging for the tubers.

Abounding from Mexico to Alaska, and from one coast to the other, this edible sedge also grows in Europe, Asia, and Africa, being cultivated in some localities for its tubers. Sweet, nutty, and milky with juice, these are clustered about the base of the plant, particularly when it grows in sandy or loose soil where a few tugs will give a hungry man his dinner. In hard dirt, the nuts are widely scattered as well as being difficult to excavate.

Except for several smaller leaves at the top of the stalk

supporting the flower clusters, all the light green, grasslike leaves of the chufa grow from the roots. These latter are comprised of long runners, terminating in little nutlike tubers. The numerous flowers grow in little, flat, yellowish spikes.

Chufa furnishes one of the wild coffees. Just separate the little tubers from their roots, wash them, and spread them out to dry. Then roast them in an oven with the door ajar until they are rich brown throughout, grind them as in the blender, and brew and serve like the store-bought beverage. So prepared, chufa tastes more like a cereal "coffee" than like the regular brew. But it is wholesome, pleasant, and it contains none of the sleep-retarding ingredients of the commercial grinds.

All you have to do is wash and eat chufas, but if you are going to have a wild-foods dinner for guests, why not go one step further and have some really different chips to serve with your dip during the cocktail hour? The chufas first have to be very well dried, as in a slow oven, then ground to powder as in the ubiquitous blender. This powder can be mixed with regular wheat flour for all sorts of appetizing vitamin-and-mineral-rich cakes, breads, and cookies.

For these chips, which resemble fat little pillows, sift together a cup of powdered chufa, a cup of all-purpose flour, 3 teaspoons baking powder, and a teaspoon of salt. Then cut in 2 tablespoons of shortening with a pastry blender or a pair of knives. Not wasting any time, work in 3/4 cup of cold water bit by bit to make your dough. Roll this out as thinly as you can. Cut into 2-inch squares and fry these one by one in hot fat. They'll puff as they bronze. If you'll turn them, the other side will expand, too. Drain the some 30 resulting chips on paper toweling. They are particularly tasty, by the way, in an avocado and tomato dip touched up with grated wild onion.

CHUFA

The Spanish make a refreshing cold drink from the chufa, enjoyed both as is and as a base for stronger concoctions. A popular alcoholic drink is made by partially freezing this beverage in the refrigerator, then adding an equal volume of light rum to make a sort of wild frozen Daiquiri. The Spanish recipe calls for soaking 1/2 pound of the well-washed tubers for 2 days. Then drain them and either mash them or put them through the blender along with 4 cups of water and 1/3 cup sugar. Strain the white, milky results, and you're in business.

Europeans in the Mediterranean area, northward as far as Great Britain, used to make a conserve of chufa that is still very much worth the trouble. Again, begin by soaking the scrubbed tubers for 2 days in cold water. You'll need a quart of the drained vegetables for this recipe.

Make a syrup by boiling together a cup of sugar, a cup of corn syrup, and 1 2/3 cups of water for 10 minutes. Add the drained chufas. Simmer, stirring occasionally, until the tubers are tender and the syrup thickened. Then take off the stove. Cover and let stand overnight. The next day, reheat to boiling. Pack the chufas in hot, sterile pint jars. Bring the liquid once more to a boil and pour it over the chufas, filling the jars to within 1/2 inch of their tops. Seal at once, cover if necessary to protect from drafts, allow to cool, label, and store.

DYE, LINIMENT, MEDICINE, COFFEE, AND DELECTABLE FOOD

SUNFLOWER

(Helianthus)

ALMOST TWO-THIRDS OF THE SUNFLOWERS THAT brighten the world, some sixty species, thrive in this country. Although they grow in every state, sunflowers spring up in greater abundance in the West, especially on the prairies. Indians used them everywhere, but it was here they were most useful to the tribes, often taking the place of maize.

However, sunflowers had, and have, many more uses. The Indians found they could boil the crushed seeds, then skim an extremely nutritious oil from the surface. This was used at mealtimes and in cooking. It was also one of this continent's earliest hair oils.

In medicine, the seeds were regarded as diuretic and the entire plant as antimalarial. The roots were boiled and the warm liquid used as a liniment. They were also supposed to be efficacious in snakebite remedies. A strong extract from wild sunflower roots was one of the original baths used to allay the severe inflammations that plague most who come in contact with poison oak and poison ivy.

Indians obtained black and purple dyes from the seeds, and a brilliant yellow dye from the plants, with which to beautify clothes, baskets, and ornaments. As if that weren't enough, the stalks can be utilized in an emergency like those of the tall, widely cultivated hemp to give delicate, silky threads.

The American wilderness is well stocked with teas, but wild coffees are scarcer. Sunflowers give one of the latter. The Senecas were among the Indians roasting sunflower seeds, after the kernels had been extracted, and pouring hot water over them to produce a coffee-like beverage.

The stately forms of wild sunflowers, reaching up to some six feet tall but seldom rivaling the size of domesticated species, are common sights in open fields and meadows and along roads. A few tolerate woodland shade. One sunflower, *Helianthus annuus*, is the state flower of Kansas, growing as far west as California and western Mexico.

Another variety, the Jerusalem artichoke, which is considered at length in *Free for the Eating*, is famous for its distinctively flavored tubers. It was cultivated by the Indians, much used by the early settlers, became a European delicacy, and is now raised for the stores while still also growing wild. Incidentally, the artichoke part of the name stems from the fact that even centuries ago the flower buds of many of the sunflowers were boiled and eaten with butter like that vegetable.

Sunflowers, which are annuals, are all relatively tall. Their stems, for the most part, are rough and stout. Their alternate, stemmed leaves, shaggy on both sides, are coarse and toothed. The blossoms are made up of many ray and disk flowers. Their total diameters in the wild plants range from about three to six inches, with disks from one to two inches broad. The disk flowers vary in color from brown and purple to yellow. The showy rays, often brilliantly turning fields into almost solid expanses of gold, usually run in number from about ten to twenty-five. Although the season of blooming is

SUNFLOWER

supposed to be later, they are sometimes seen blossoming gaily in early spring.

The agreeably oily seeds of the wild sunflowers are important to such game birds as snipe, quail, grouse, partridge, dove and pheasant. Antelope, deer, and moose dine on the plants.

Sunflower seeds are nutritious and, particularly when roasted in an oven or beside a campfire, delicious. Because the tedious job of shelling does not fit in with the high-speed tempo of American living, we enjoy them far less in the United States than, for example, do millions in eastern Europe. However, there continues to be a steady demand for the little bags of toasted, salted nuts at candy counters across the nation.

The fact remains that in an emergency the wild seeds could make all the difference. This would be true whether or not you just ate them raw or, as Lewis and Clark found the Indians doing along the Missouri River, pounded the kernels to a fine meal to drink with water, to make into bread, to stir into soups as thickening, or to mix with marrow.

This last is especially tasty, besides being of important interest from a survival standpoint. The mineral-rich marrow found in the bones of animals that were in good physical condition at their demise is not surpassed by any other natural food in caloric strength. What is, at the same time, the most delectable of tidbits is too often wasted by the common practice of roasting such bones until they are on the point of crumbling or of boiling them for hours. A more conservative procedure is to crack them near the onset, with two stones if nothing handier is available, or to poke out the soft vascular tissue with the flattened end of a stick. The less the marrow is then cooked, the better it will remain as far as nutrition is concerned.

To shell sunflower seeds in quantity, first break them up, as with a rolling pin, hammer, or food chopper. Then scatter the results in a large container filled with water. Stir vigorously so as to bring all the kernels in contact with the fluid and to break the surface tension. The kernels will sink to the bottom. The shells will remain floating, for use as a wild coffee if you want. The nuts can then be briefly dried and roasted, as in an open oven pan, and used in any recipe calling for nuts. Or the entire mass of kernels can be ground or pounded into a fine meal.

One of the Indian ways of making sunflower cakes is still a good one. For this recipe, you'll need 2 cups of hulled sunflower seeds and 2 cups of water. Put the two together in a saucepan, add 1 1/2 teaspoons salt, cover, and simmer for an hour, stirring occasionally. Then, unless you started with a meal, puree the mixture in your blender. Allow to cool.

Mix in about 4 tablespoons of cornmeal, a scattering at a time, until you have a dough firm enough to shape. Mold this into round, flat cakes about 2 inches wide. Get 2/3 cup of shortening or cooking oil warming in a frypan. When it is hot enough to make a drop of water dance, put the cakes carefully in with a spatula. Turning, bronze them well on both sides. Then drain on absorbent paper. Most prefer these hot, but they're still tasty cold.

THE PLEASANTLY ASSERTIVE CONDIMENT THAT'S SO GOOD

HORSERADISH

(Armoracia)

THERE IS LITTLE COMPARISON BETWEEN THE freshly grated horseradish you can prepare yourself, using the wild roots and lemon juice instead of the commonly employed wine vinegar, and that from a store. Mouth-tickling horseradish, popular the world over, has been used as a food seasoning for centuries.

The perennial horseradish, regrowing in the same places for dozens of years and spreading where there is sufficient moisture, came to the New World from England. Originally planted about the cabins and other buildings of northeastern United States and southern Canada, it has thrived and dispersed until it now grows wild throughout much of the same general area. The nose-stinging, eye-watering white roots, so good when used in moderation with less tasty foods, are edible the year around.

The small white flowers of the horseradish, like those of all other members of the mustard family, have just four petals. They grow in short-stemmed, loosely branched clusters. Although seeds are seldom produced, there are the occasional round pods, each of which is divided into two cells with perhaps four to six seeds in each.

Numerous large leaves grow from the root on strong, long

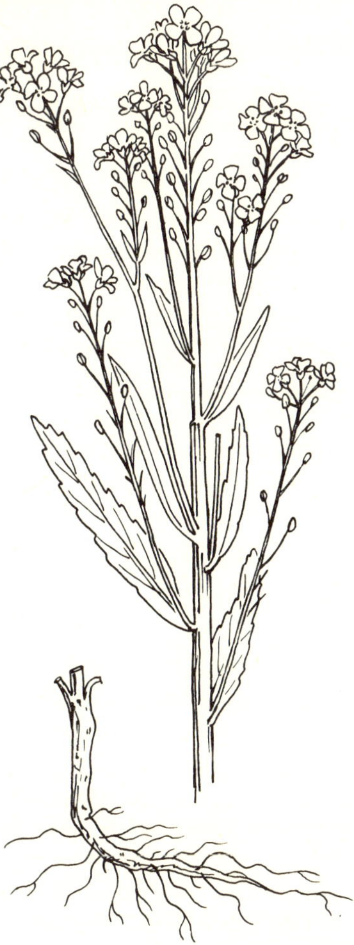

HORSERADISH

stalks. These leaves, often six inches wide and nearly twice as long, have wavy, scalloped edges. The much smaller, stemless leaves that grow directly from a smooth, round, erect, central spike, often several feet long, are oblong and serrated.

The leaves when tender in the spring make greens that are tastier than most when dropped into a small amount of boiling salted water, cooked uncovered only until tender, and then served immediately with a crowning pat of butter or margarine.

But it is for its heartily peppery roots that horseradish has been famous for thousands of years. These fleshy roots, sometimes as long as a foot and as thick as one or two inches, are tapering, conical at the top, and many times abruptly branched near the end. They are white both within and without. When bruised or scraped, they give off a strongly pungent odor. When a particle is transferred to the tongue, it is immediately hot and biting.

The simplest way to prepare this masterful condiment for the table is by scraping some of the scrubbed root into a small dish, then stirring in fresh lemon juice to taste. Or you can use wine vinegar, instead.

Then there are innumerable refinements, the easiest of which is to add a small amount of sugar to the original mixture, again by taste. In any event, for the most pleasing results make only small amounts of the sauce at a time, an easy thing to do as horseradish roots can be freshly gathered the year around.

Keep the sauce covered when not in use, preferably in a tightly closed jar or bottle. You may want to keep this in the refrigerator. For best results, however, it should be allowed to return to room temperature before being used. Otherwise, part of its taste-tingling piquancy will be trapped by the cold, and more will have to be used to achieve the same result.

Grated horseradish and sour cream make a combination that really brings out the flavor of game meats such as roast moose and bear, not to forget good honest beef. Two parts of sour cream by volume to 1 part of horseradish blend excellently.

You can use regular cream, too. Mix 2 teaspoons of finely grated horseradish with 1/4 teaspoon salt and 2 tablespoons water. Then whip 1/2 cup of heavy cream. Stir the first mixture into the cream. Allow to stand half an hour before using.

Here's a way to make horseradish sauce more pleasantly assertive. Begin by whipping the same 1/2 cup of heavy cream. When it starts to thicken, gradually tip in a tablespoon of lemon juice. Once everything thickens, add 1/2 teaspoon paprika, 1/4 teaspoon dry mustard, and 1/4 teaspoon salt. Then fold in 2 tablespoons of freshly grated horseradish. Before putting on the table, allow to stand a half-hour until the flavors can affirm themselves.

Freshly grated horseradish will also do much for sandwiches and for small crisp crackers—tidbits that will arouse the appetite even more if decorated with slices of pimento-stuffed olives. For this spread, cream butter or margarine with an equal volume of horseradish. Then gradually add a little lemon juice, salt, paprika, and, if you want, sugar to taste. If you ever tire of this, substitute cream cheese for the butter or margarine. Or use mayonnaise for the base.

Besides enjoying horseradish roots and leaves, pioneers used to apply the freshly scraped roots externally as they would mustard plasters. Horseradish was also used as an internal medicine, a teaspoon of the scraped root to a cup of boiling water. This was allowed to cool. One or two cupfuls were then drunk throughout the day, several sips at a time, as a stimulant to the stomach.

THE NOBLEST OF ALL WILD FRUITS

APPLE

(Malus)

"THE TIME FOR WILD APPLES IS the last of October and the first of November," averred an early expert on the subject, Henry David Thoreau. "They then get to be palatable, vivacious and inspiring, for they ripen late.

"To appreciate the wild and sharp flavors of these October fruits, it is necessary that you be breathing the sharp October or November air. The outdoor air and exercise which the walker gets give a different tone to his palate, and he craves a fruit which the sedentary would call harsh and crabbed.

"This noblest of fruits must be eaten in the fields, when your system is all aglow with exercise," Thoreau said, "when the frosty weather nips your fingers, the wind rattles the bare boughs or rustles the few remaining leaves, and the jay is heard screaming around. What is sour in the house a bracing walk makes sweet. Some of these apples might be labelled, 'To be eaten in the wind'."

Apples, natives of Asia and Europe, were not brought to Massachusetts until some nine years after the arrival of the Pilgrims, but they soon escaped into the wilderness. Nearly 200 years ago, the pioneer preacher named John Chapman, better known as Johnny Appleseed, traveled some 100,000 miles between Massachusetts and Missouri planting seeds and seedlings. Apples and crab apples *(Pyrus)* now grow wild in every state of the Union.

Most of these are only occasionally to be relished raw, although they cook up all the better for that. However, as Thoreau noted more than a century ago, "Who knows but this chance wild fruit, planted by a cow or a bird on some remote and rocky hillside, may be the choicest of its kind. It was thus the Porter and the Baldwin grow. Every wild apple shrub excites our expectation thus, somewhat as every wild child it is, perhaps, a prince in disguise."

Everyone knows the apple. Even though your yellow-green find may be little more than an inch in diameter, and hard and sour to boot, very few wild fruits are as quickly gathered, and their very tartness and firmness lend themselves to some of the finest apple dishes you have ever eaten. The flowers of the apple are perhaps the most beautiful of any tree. The scent of both them and the later developing fruit has a piquancy unequaled in any costly perfume.

Deer, bears, raccoons, and foxes are among the wild animals who seek out apples. Apple buds are a favorite winter sustenance of the ruffed grouse. Pheasant, quail, and prairie chicken dine well on fruit, seeds, and buds.

The Iroquois, employing wild apples and maple syrup, made an applesauce that was all the more flavorsome because the fruit was used unpeeled. With the help of the kitchen blender, you can do an even smoother job of this today. Cut up the apples first, removing the cores. Barely cover with water, bring to a simmer, and cook with only an occasional bubble ascending to the top until the fruit is soft. Transfer at once to the blender, whirling it in this until nothing remains of the peel but the savor and color.

Then add sugar to taste, preferably stopping short of

obliterating all the tartness. You may also like what a little cinnamon and lemon juice will do for applesauce. A bit of salt will help bring out the deliciousness, too. Much depends on the particular wild fruit. Many like this best when it is warm, perhaps with a splash of cream.

If you can beat the deer and other forest folk to them, you sometimes come upon wild apples plump and sweet enough for baking. Carefully cut out the cores. Arrange the fruit in a pan. Then fill each hollow as nearly as you can with 2 tablespoons brown sugar, a teaspoon butter or margarine, 1/8 teaspoon nutmeg, and a small pinch of salt. Pour 1/2 inch of boiling water into the bottom of the pan. Bake in a moderate 375-degree oven, frequently spooning the thickening syrup over the fruit, until a testing fork indicates that the apples are soft. This dish, best hot, calls for either fresh cream or liberal scoops of vanilla ice cream.

Another wild apple dessert that is good hot with cream, although in the woods evaporated milk chilled in a brook will do, is apple slump. This recipe is geared to 6 cups of wild apples, pared, cored, and thinly sliced. The amount of sugar will depend on the tartness of the particular fruit. Start with 1 cup of sugar, also adding a teaspoon of cinnamon and 1/2 cup of water. Bring to a simmer in a large saucepan with a tightly fitting cover. Now correct the sweetening.

Sift 2 cups of sifted all-purpose flour, 2 1/2 teaspoons baking powder, 1 teaspoon sugar, and 1/2 teaspoon salt. Using a pastry blender or 2 knives, cut in 1/3 cup of shortening until the texture of the mixture is similar to that of coarse cornmeal. Using a fork, stir in enough milk bit by bit to make a soft dough. Drop this from a tablespoon atop the hot apples, cover tightly, and simmer over low heat without lifting the cover for a half-hour. You may occasionally like to vary this

APPLE

recipe by cutting 1/2 cup grated sharp American cheese into the flour mixture along with the shortening.

One way to appreciate wild apples with their, according to Thoreau, "wild flavors of the Muse," is in what back in New England natives used to call apple snow. Peel, core, and slice your apples. Simmer them in just enough water to cover until they are soft enough to press through a sieve. Sweeten them to taste with a minimum of white sugar and allow to cool. For each cup of apple, fold in a stiffly whipped egg white. Serve either with cream or whole milk.

For something special in the way of dessert, sift 2 cups of all-purpose flour into a mixing bowl. Press a hollow in the center and add a stick of melted butter or margarine, 2 egg yolks, 3 tablespoons sugar, and 1/8 teaspoon salt. Blend thoroughly, moistening with a little cold water if necessary. Then wad into a ball, wrap in foil or waxed paper or place in a covered bowl, and refrigerate for an hour.

In the meantime, chop 2 1/2 cups pared and cored wild apples. Brown them in a frypan, along with 1/2 stick of butter or margarine, with 1/2 cup seedless raisins, 2 tablespoons heavy rum, 1 teaspoon cinnamon, and about a cup of sugar—however much the particular fruit needs.

Then roll out the dough very thinly. Cover it with the fruit and roll it up tightly. Brush it with melted butter or margarine, sprinkle lightly with sugar and cinnamon, place in a well-greased pan, and bake in a moderate 350-degree oven for about a half-hour or until the pastry is done. Cut into slices and, for a taste treat, serve with wild applesauce.

Wild apples really lend themselves to this sour cream pie. Make enough pastry for a 9-inch double-crust pie by sifting together 2 cups of all-purpose flour and a teaspoon of salt. Using a pastry blender or 2 knives, cut in 2/3 cup shortening until the mixture is the texture of large peas. Stir in about 1/3 cup cold water, a bit at a time, until you have a ball of dough. Lightly roll out half of this 1/8-inch thick and line a greased, deep pie pan with it. Slice 1/2 stick of butter or margarine over this pastry and scatter a tablespoon of sugar and a teaspoon of flour over it.

Core, pare, and chop enough wild apples to fill the pan, about 5 cups. Combine a cup of sugar, 1 teaspoon cinnamon, 1/4 teaspoon each of ginger, nutmeg, and salt, and 1/8 teaspoon cloves. Flatten a layer of apples over the bottom, sprinkle with the sugar mixture, and repeat until everything is used. Pour a cup of sour cream over the mound of fruit. Top with 1/2-inch strips of crust, moistening the rim of the lower pastry with water and pressing the ribbons firmly to it. Slice the remaining 1/2 stick of butter or margarine over everything.

Bake in a preheated hot 450-degree oven for 10 minutes. Then lower the temperature to a moderate 350 degrees and continue cooking another half-hour or until the apples are tender and the crust is golden brown on top. For that extra touch, serve this with thin, freshly sliced cuts of sharp American cheese.

THE PICKLE THAT IS ALSO AN EMERGENCY FISHING LINE

GIANT KELP

(Nereocystis)

IF YOU LIVE OR VACATION WHERE giant kelp grows, this abundant marine alga, which often thrives in beds acres wide, makes unusual and excellent pickles.

Giant kelp has round, hollow stalks up to about seventy-five feet long, gradually widening from less than one-half inch at the base to perhaps four inches at the top and ending in a floating round bulb which may be up to eight inches in diameter. Two rows of narrow, leathery, leaflike blades, ten to thirty feet long, stem from the bulbs. These blades float on the ocean surface, and on the Pacific Coast from Mexico to Alaska you can often watch sea lions, whales, and sometimes sea otters swimming among them.

The long, hollow stalks, used by the Indians of southeastern Alaska as fishing lines for deep-sea angling, may be collected during June; July, and August, when they are at their prime. Although it is preferable to use only the ones rooted to the bottom, fresh stalks are also common along the beaches, especially after storms.

The kelp is washed, peeled, and used the same as green cucumbers or tomatoes for relish and pickles. It may also be used like watermelon rind for preserving.

For some memorable sweet sea pickles, you'll need 4 pounds giant kelp, 3 1/2 cups sugar, 2 cups white vinegar, 1 cup

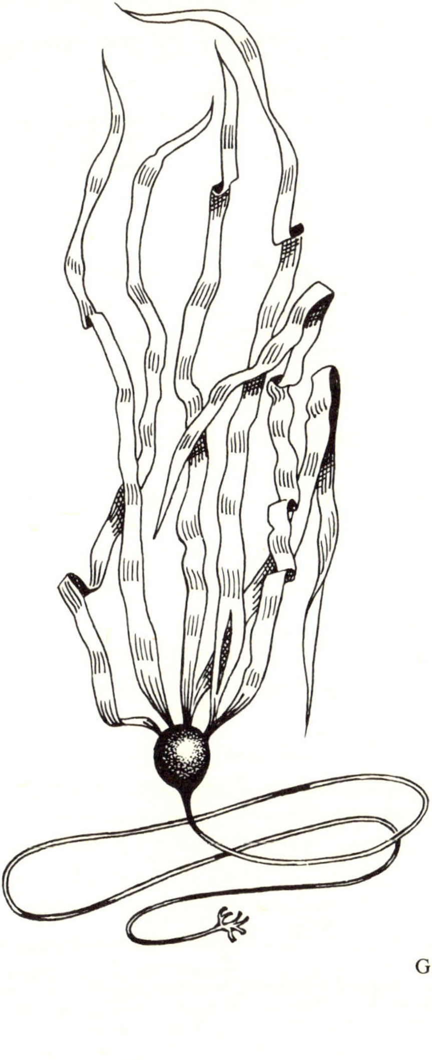

GIANT KELP

salt, 1/2 teaspoon alum, 1/2 teaspoon oil of cloves, 1/2 teaspoon oil of cinnamon, and water.

Cut the stalks into 12-inch lengths and split the bulbs. Using a vegetable parer, remove the dark surface layer and discard. Keep the pieces covered in a brine solution, 1 cup of salt to 2 gallons of water, for 2 hours. After the giant kelp is taken out of the brine, wash it thoroughly with cold water.

Then cut it into 1-inch cubes. Soak these in a solution of 1/2 teaspoon of alum to 2 quarts of cold water for 15 minutes. Drain, wash in cold water, and redrain. Drop the cubes into an enamel kettle and cover them with boiling water. Simmer only until a few test cubes can be easily pierced with a fork. Then drain again.

Combine the sugar, vinegar, and oils. Simmer this for 2 minutes and then pour over the cooked kelp. Let stand overnight in the enamel kettle or in a crock. In the morning, drain and save the syrup. Reheat the kelp to the boiling point with just enough water to prevent sticking, pour off the water, recover with the syrup, and allow to set another 24 hours. On the third morning, heat both kelp and syrup to the boiling point, and seal immediately in 3 hot, sterilized pint jars.

Whole spices, tied in small bags, may be used instead, but the cubes will not then remain so nearly transparently clear. A conservative amount of green food coloring may be put in to make the pickles brighter. If you don't mind sacrificing a certain amount of crispness, omit the salt and alum solutions, merely soaking the kelp in cold water, rinsing, and then cooking until tender.

ACTUAL FORESTS OF FOOD

POPLAR

(Populus)

WHEN WOOD SMOKE LIFTS AMONG POPLAR in patterns as primitive as those formed there other days by frost crystals, have you sometimes found yourself wishing you could taste peace and quiet and solitude long enough to find out how good they—and you—really are?

Maybe you've even put into words this natural yearning of that portion of our most primitive ancestor which survives within us. Circumstances may conceivably be such for anybody, whether because of misadventure or storm or man-loosed disaster, that tomorrow a man may be alone in the wilderness and compelled to rely solely on his own ingenuity and resourcefulness for survival.

Most individuals worry that, if forced to shift for themselves in the unfrequented farther places, they would starve. Yet there are actual forests of food.

The poplar's sweetish, starchy sap layer is edible both raw and cooked. This lies between the wood of trunks, branches, and twigs and the outside bark, the latter being intensely bitter with salicin, which for some reason is relished by moose, beaver, and rabbit and is an ingredient in some tonics concocted for the benefit of mankind.

All three animals chaw poplar bark, and poplar trunks

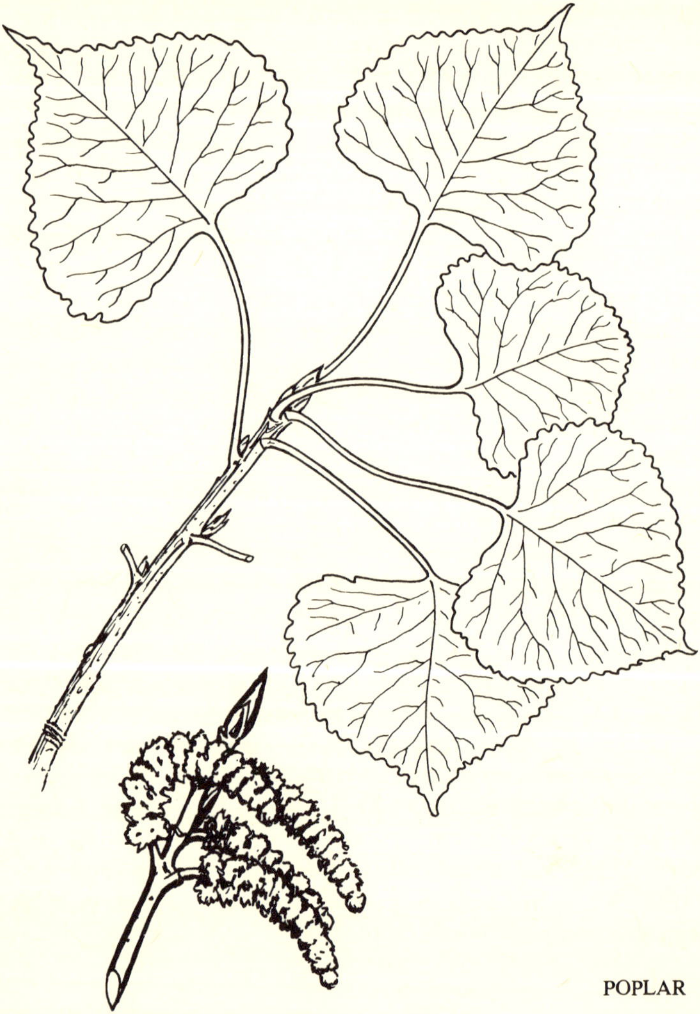

POPLAR

and branches are common in beaver dams and houses. Deer, elk, and mountain sheep browse on the twigs and foliage. Grouse, prairie chickens, and quail are among the game birds relying on buds, catkins, and seeds.

One of the most common trees on the continent, the life-giving poplar grows about as far north as any other on the great barrens of Canada. Cottonwoods as well as aspens are poplars. On the other hand, the so-called yellow poplar of the Southeast is not a poplar at all. In numerous northern areas, poplars quickly spring up in burns and clearings.

The poplars, members of the great willow family which has saved more than one man from starving, have alternate leaves with toothed and sometimes lobed edges. The stems are long and slender, occasionally being definitely flattened. The branches are characteristically brittle and, breaking easily from trunks and big limbs, make excellent firewood for lone campfires, burning with a clean, medicinal odor.

Pollen fills the wind when the flowers, growing in drooping spikelike clusters, appear in the first warm weather of spring before the light green leaves blaze forth, like pale green fire crowning the forest. The cottony aspect of the later splitting capsules of seeds, each with its long, fibrous hairs, has brought the name "cottonwood" to some species.

The soft formative tissue between wood and bark can be scraped off and eaten on the spot. One of the modern ways of obtaining such nourishment is in tea. It can also be cut into strips or chunks and cooked like noodles in soups and stews. Dried and powdered, it is a flour additive and substitute. No matter how it is eaten, however, it can by itself keep you going for weeks.

THE WILD FRUIT THAT WON HOMER'S PRAISE

HACKBERRY

(Celtis)

HOMER ASSERTED THAT THE THIN, SUGARY pulp of the hackberry proved so delectable to the ancients that those who ate it forgot their native countries. Eight of the world's some fifty to seventy-five species (depending on the botanist) are native to the United States. These trees and shrubs range over a large proportion of the nation in habitats varying from wet, swampy spots and stream banks to rich, rocky hillsides and hardwood forests. They are frequently planted for shade and decoration. The local name of sugarberry recognizes the pleasant, wholesome sweetness of the fruit.

Wildlife feasts on the fruit of the hackberry, also known as the nettle tree and as the hoop ash. Cedar waxwings flit among the branches as long as the last frost-sweetened drupe remains. Such upland game birds as quail, turkeys, pigeons, and doves become more palatable on a similar diet. So do beavers, opossums, raccoons, and squirrels. Both mule and white-tailed deer browse on the twigs and foliage.

Even the botanist has considerable trouble in distinguishing all the species of the hackberry. Generally they are shrubs or small trees with alternate leaves, typically lopsided at the base. Three prominent veins rise from the top of the short stem. So-called witches'-broom, dense clusters of small twigs,

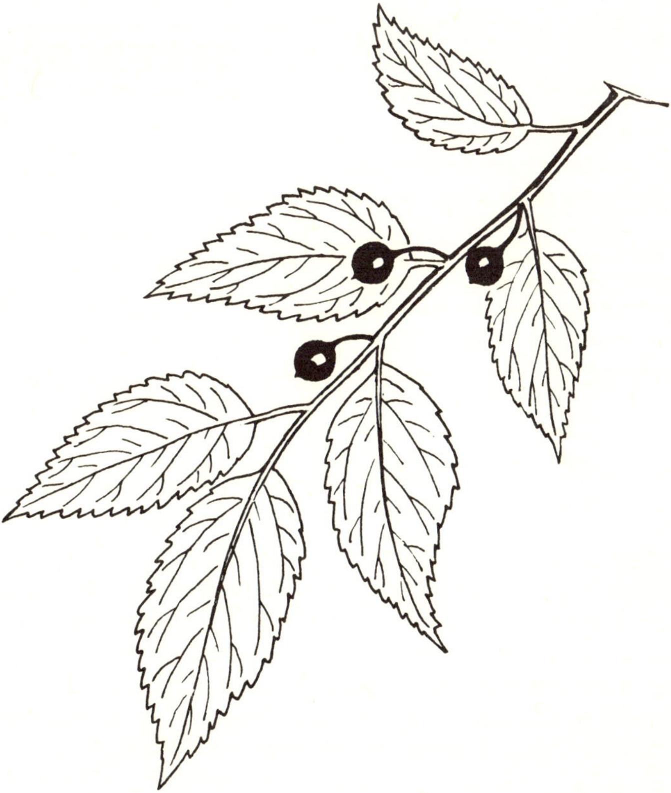

HACKBERRY

frequently appear in the hackberry, also commonly distinguished by warty outgrowths of a corky nature on the bark.

The flowers, small and inconspicuous, blossom out in the junction between the leaf stalk and the branch at the same time the leaves are developing in the spring. These flowers are followed by berries that are actually drupes; each drupe consists of a sweet, thin pulp covering a large, round seed. About the size of peas, these drupes vary in color from orange-red and yellowish to dark purple.

Ripening in September or October but often persisting on the branches until well into winter and becoming even more sweet with cold weather, hackberries, although dry, will pleasantly take the edge off hunger. They are an important survival food.

Some Indians, after feasting on the pulp, used to dry the large pits and pound them into fine bits for seasoning meats. The soft white kernels, exposed by cracking the outer shell, are sweet and somewhat datelike in flavor.

THE ASPARAGUS RIVAL THAT GROWS FROM COAST TO COAST

MILKWEED

(Asclepias)

JUST A FEW WEEKS AFTER *Free for the Eating* had reached the bookstores, I received a letter from a reader who was disappointed that we had omitted milkweed. This, she said, she always gathered in the spring "when it is just coming up—when it is about the size of asparagus as we get it in the markets...I wish to say that this milkweed, cooked with a small piece of salt pork as we'd cook dandelions, is as delicious as any asparagus I have ever eaten and even tastes somewhat like it."

One of the many interesting things about this letter is that the "old lady," as she described herself, who wrote it lives only several miles from where I grew up in Massachusetts. Space limitation was the only reason, of course, I left milkweed out of the earlier book, as it is one of the most delicious wild edibles of which I know. I, too, have enjoyed it many times.

Although milkweed grows from coast to coast and was long used by the Indians, it is the common milkweed, *Asclepias syriaca,* with which many are most familiar. This native perennial, thriving from the Maritimes to Saskatchewan and south to Kansas and the Carolinas, has stout stems reaching from two to five feet high.

This milkweed is abundant in meadows, old fields, marshes, and along roadsides, where in the fall its seeds with their familiar parachutes waft away by the thousands into the wind. These, plus a milky juice—latex, the subject of numerous experiments seeking a native rubber—are the plant's two predominant characteristics. However, these edibles should never be identified by this milky sap alone.

The leaves of this branchless edible grow in opposite pairs. Their short stems, like the stalks, are stout and sturdy. From four to nine inches long, and about half as wide, these oblong to ovate leaves taper at both top and bottom. They have wide central ribs.

The clusters of numerous tiny flowers have a memorable fragrance. They vary in color from greenish lilac to almost white. Each of the components of the delicate blossoms, which are deadly traps to many of the insects that seek their nectar, is divided into five parts. They eventually produce large green pods, some three to five inches long. The warty coverings of these finally split, exposing silk-tufted seeds.

As already considered, young milkweed sprouts, when up to some eight inches tall, are excellent asparagus substitutes—if "substitute" is the right word, their being so regally satisfying in their own right. Then the young leaves provide cooking greens. The flower buds are a delicacy. Running the sprouts a close second, and even surpassing them in some estimations, are the firm, young pods. If they are at all elastic in your fingers, however, the silken wings of the seeds have developed too far to make for good eating.

There is one thing to keep in mind, however. All parts of the plant are bitter with the pervasive latex. However, this is

MILKWEED

readily soluble in water. Put your milkweed—whether sprouts, young leaves, flower buds, or seedpods—all ready for cooking, in a saucepan. Cover it with boiling water, bring again to a boil over high heat, and pour off. Do this at least once again, maybe more times, depending on your palate. To some, a slight bitterish tinge is invigorating. In any event, finally recover with boiling water, add a bit of salt, and simmer until tender. This may require a bit longer than expected, as milkweed takes more cooking than most other greens. Serve with margarine or butter melting on top.

I've also used the similar *Asclepias speciosa* with its purplish flowers on the western side of the continent, from British Columbia to California.

The tough fibers of the mature stalks of this milkweed were employed by the Indians for making string and rope and for coarse weaving. The milky juice was applied to warts and to ringworm infections, as well as to ordinary sores and cuts. The exquisitely packed ripe seeds were gathered just before soaring and skittering over the landscape, their hairy protuberances burned off, and the remainder ground into a salve for sores. These seeds were also boiled in a minimum of water and the concentrated liquid applied to draw the poison out of rattlesnake bites.

Besides serving as a cough medicine, a hot beverage made by steeping the roots was taken to bring out the rash in measles. Externally, it was supposed to help rheumatism. The root, mashed with water, was applied as a poultice to reduce swelling.

Once the shoots are more than eight inches tall and too old to eat, the bottom leaves can no longer be used but the young top leaves are still tender and tasty before the green flowers. These are fine mixed with young dandelion leaves, although they are good by themselves, too. Then there are the buds themselves, prepared and cooked the same way. Finally, the young pods are fine served on the side with roast or steak, or you may like what they can do for a stew.

Getting back to the blossoms, the Indians are supposed to have used them for sweetening on summer mornings, shaking the dew-laden nectar onto their foods before this dampness evaporated in the heat of the day. This has never worked for me, however, perhaps because I've become too lazy too soon.

VEGETABLE, FRUIT, AND NUT—ALL IN ONE

KNOTWEED

(Polygonum)

SOME THIRTY OR SO SPECIES OF knotweed occur in practically every part of the United States. Grouse, mourning doves, pheasants, quail, prairie chickens, woodcocks, and partridges devour the rather large, dark seeds. Antelope and deer eat the plants.

Man has long dined on the knotweed, using various members of the family as vegetable, fruit, and even as nut. The fleshy and starchy rootstocks of the *Polygonum bistorta* in British Columbia and the Yukon are cooked and eaten as a substitute for nuts because of their almond-like taste, and in the Arctic south to New England and Colorado, the raw roots of the *Polygonum bistorta* are enjoyed for the same nutlike characteristic.

It is the Japanese knotweed, *Polygonum cuspidatum*, with which many are most familiar. This is well known, although not always by name, from North Carolina to Missouri, north to southern Canada, growing in large, coarse stands from about three to eight feet high. The enlarged joints of the stalks are encased with thin, papery sheaths. When these hollow stalks die, they form bamboo-like thickets which clack and rattle in the wind and which serve to identify the young,

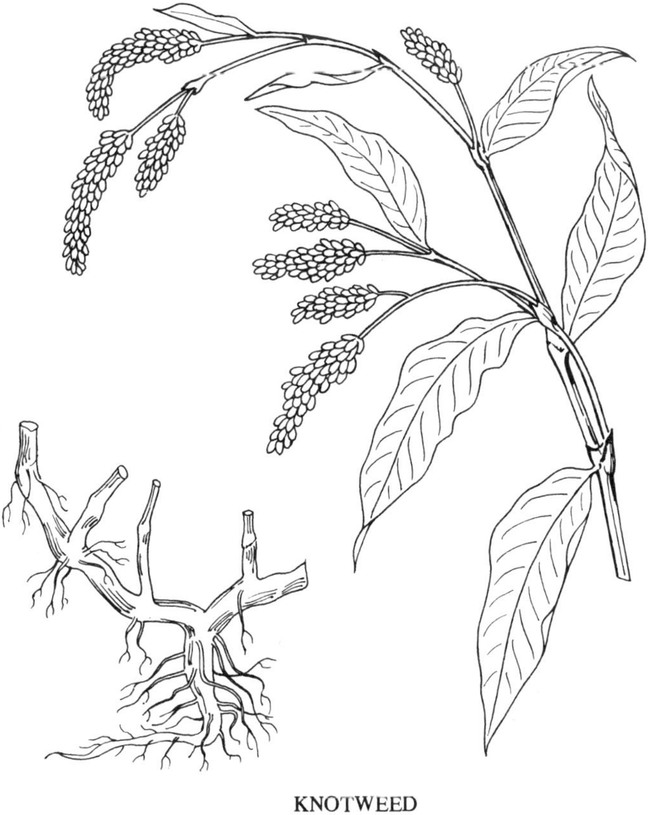

KNOTWEED

edible sprouts when, somewhat resembling asparagus in shape although not in taste, these shoot up lustily in the spring.

The stemmed green leaves of this knotweed are roundly egg-shaped, being broad at their bases but rather abruptly pointed at their tips. The whitish green flowers, each with its five outer lobes, grow profusely in branching clusters that appear in the angles between leaves and stalk.

Knotweed shoots, before the leaves start to unfurl, are delicately delicious when some twelve to fifteen inches high. They cook up much more rapidly than asparagus. Three or four minutes in boiling salted water will do the job. Their toothsome acidity is then brought out with melted butter or margarine. Its shoots also taste good cold with mayonnaise. Both ways they go well with hot buttered toast.

To lift this wild edible to a heavenly level, cook and drain enough for four. Lay in a well-greased casserole, strew to taste with pepper and salt, and mix gently with 1/2 cup cream. Roof with 2/3 cup of fresh white bread crumbs mixed with 2 tablespoons of melted butter or margarine. For a variation on occasion, sprinkle with 1/4 cup grated Parmesan cheese. In either event, bake in a preheated hot 400-degree oven until the top is golden brown. Try this sometime with cold ham, hard-cooked eggs, and sliced tomatoes.

One of the knotweeds in Alaska, *Polygonum alaskanum*, is called wild rhubarb because the young stems in early spring are used the same way as domesticated rhubarb. This will work, too, with Japanese knotweed. First, carefully peel the outer skin from the thinly fleshed stalks. Then cut into segments. Four cups of these, plus a cup of sugar and 1/8 teaspoon nutmeg, will give you enough tart sauce for four. If you'll let this stand a few minutes, it'll quickly simmer to softness in its own juice. Many like it hot with a little cream. It's tangy ice cold, too.

SPRING TONIC AND BOYHOOD FAVORITE

SLIPPERY ELM

(Ulmus)

POUR A CUP OF BOILING WATER over a teaspoon of the shredded inner bark of the slippery elm. Cover and allow to steep until cool. Then add lemon juice and sugar to taste, and you'll have some of the famous slippery elm tea of pioneer days, still highly regarded as a spring tonic and as a plain pleasant drink in some parts of the country.

The slippery elm—also known as the red, gray, moose, and rock elm—abounds on bottomlands and on rich, rocky inclines in company with other hardwoods. A medium-sized tree, generally some forty to seventy feet tall with a trunk diameter from about one to three feet, it grows from Maine and southern Quebec to North Dakota, south to eastern Texas and northern Florida. Spreading branches provide broad, open, flattish crowns.

The sharply toothed leaves, scratchy above and downy beneath, grow on short, hairy, stout stems. Growing from woolly, egg-shaped, blunt buds about one-quarter of an inch long, the leaves become unsymmetrical, four to eight inches long, and from two to three inches across the middle, where they are usually broadest. Dark green and dull, lighter on their under portions, they turn to beautiful masses of golden yellow in autumn. The bark is either grayish or dark reddish brown, becoming divided by shallow fissures and mottled by

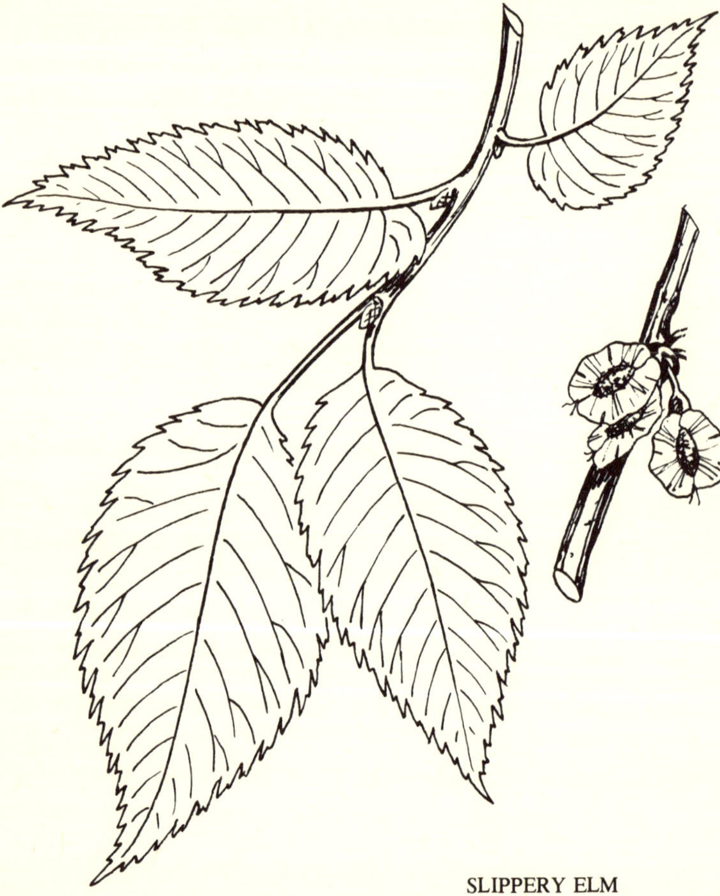

SLIPPERY ELM

large, loose scales. The hairy twigs, incidentally, turn out to be mucilaginous when chewed.

The inner bark of branches, trunk, and root is extremely mucilaginous. Thick and fragrant, it is still widely gathered in the spring, when because of the rising sap, trees peel more readily. This whitish inner bark is then dried as in a garret or a warm, half-open oven, then powdered as in the kitchen blender. It has demulcent and emollient, as well as nutritive, properties. Medically, it is still sometimes used for dysentery, diseases of the urinary passages, and bronchitis. For external application, the finely ground or powdered bark is mixed with enough hot water to make a pasty mass and used as a poultice for inflammations, boils, etc., and also in the form of both rectal and vaginal suppositories. More simply, the tea described in the first paragraph is sometimes used for coughs due to colds, one or two cupfuls a day, several cold sips at a time.

Many boys chew this intriguing bark. The Indians used it for food, some of them boiling it with the tallow they rendered from buffalo fat. In an emergency, it will provide life-saving nourishment today, and not at all unpleasantly, either raw or boiled.

THE WILD FLOWER THAT COULD SAVE YOUR LIFE

JACK-IN-THE-PULPIT

(Arisaema)

MANY INDIANS RELIED ON THE DRIED and powdered roots of the familiar jack-in-the-pulpit for flour. Today, however, this edible has its principal value as an emergency food, especially for people stranded in one place for a long time. Widely known and easily recognizable, it can then be a lifesaver.

Indian turnip, wake-robin, and dragonroot are among the local names for this North and South American member of the great *Arum* family, used for food by people the world over. Both the leaves and the bright red fruit are eaten by the ring-necked pheasant and the wild turkey.

In the moist, sequestered woodlands of April and May, the jack-in-the-pulpit preaches his silent sermon to a congregation of wild violets and other spring neighbors. Unmistakable, the brown, green, and purplish "pulpit" is a striped two- to four-inch spathe terminating with a hood over the top. The "preacher" is a clublike spadix, two or three inches long, with small greenish yellow flowers, occasionally varying greatly in hues and in brightness, near its base.

The plant, growing in rich woods from the Maritime Provinces to Florida, west to Minnesota and Louisiana, becomes from one to three feet high. The two leaves, growing on long stems, are each composed of three egg-shaped, sometimes

JACK-IN-THE-PULPIT

lobed, pointed leaflets. Green clusters of berries become handsome scarlet masses that brighten the dark woods in late August.

All parts of the plant, especially the round roots, will burn the mouth like liquid fire if eaten raw. Many youngsters used to have a standard ceremony for initiating newcomers to town, and perhaps still do. This consisted of offering the tenderfoot the tiniest morsel of what they claimed was the finest delicacy their woods had to offer. At first contact, this innocent-looking tidbit was palatable enough. But then the taste became as bitingly hot as a teaspoon of red pepper. This burning sensation, which was followed by inflammation and tenderness, seemed to permeate every part of tongue, mouth, and throat and to linger for hours, although cold milk did appear to allay it some.

The wonder is that aborigines the world over have learned to rid arum roots of this corrosive acridness and thus capitalize upon their nutritious, delicate, white starchiness. Boiling won't do it! Drying will. The fastest way to do this is by roasting. The simplest method is just to cut the fresh roots into very thin slices, then set these aside in a dry place for upwards of three months. They then provide pleasant snacks, either as is or with a potato chip dip. Or you can crumble the crisp slices into flour and use it in regular recipes, preferably half and half with wheat flour.

Jack-in-the-pulpits and hazelnuts, often growing in the same habitats, go together in the following cookies which always seem to call for seconds and thirds whenever guests get their first samples of them. Beat 2 egg yolks until thick. Add, bit by bit, a cup of brown sugar and beat that in well. Then mix in a cup of chopped hazelnuts and a scant 1/8 teaspoon salt.

Beat the 2 egg whites until they form peaks and fold them

in. Sift together 3 tablespoons jack-in-the-pulpit flour and 3 tablespoons all-purpose flour. Stir that in. Distribute by the teaspoonful on cooky sheets or heavy foil, press gently flat with a spatula, transfer to a preheated 350-degree oven, and bake about 7 minutes or until firm. After they have cooled, keep the 4 dozen or so cookies in a closed container for as long as they last, which isn't likely to be long.

Once the fire had been taken out of them, jack-in-the-pulpit roots were also held to be medicinally valuable. One prescription for spasms of asthma consisted of a handful of the dried and chipped roots, aged for three days in a quart of whisky. Even then, the dosage was conservative. It was a single tablespoonful twice a day.

THE GREEN THAT SOME HUNTERS ARE GLAD TO KNOW

ROCK CRESS

(Arabis)

THE FINEST BIG GAME HUNTING AND freshwater fishing in this hemisphere is now in the Far North. But this is also the land of the great hunger. Storm, ice, fog, or other conditions can delay scheduled plane or boat pickups. Too, fresh greens are often lacking in regular food supplies. There may be a time when you'll be glad to know rock cress.

This grows in Alaska, on the islands of the Bering Sea and the Aleutians, and in the Yukon. Alpine cress (*Arabis alpina*), which is similar, thrives in the eastern Arctic, south to Newfoundland and the Gaspé Peninsula. Both are seen on ledges, cliffs, gravelly shores, cool rocks, and along the banks of roads and streams.

Rock cress has a slender stem, often much branched from the base, up to about a foot high. Narrow, alternate, sometimes toothed leaves, gradually tapering at the bottom but not clasping the stalk, are scattered along the stem. Lobed basal leaves, up to an inch and one-half long, form characteristic rosettes. Long, loose clusters of pretty white flowers, each with four petals, appear in the spring. These develop into slender, long seedpods.

The somewhat radish-like flavor of the rosettes, gathered

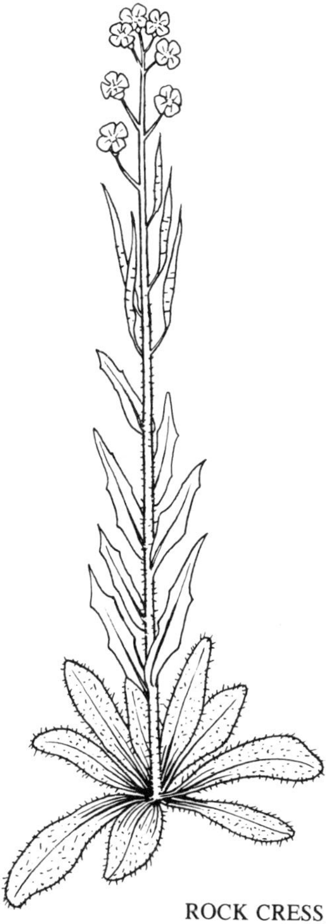

ROCK CRESS

while tender, will enhance tossed salads as well as cook up into tasty greens. The flowers, too, are edible, but the stem leaves are apt to be bitter.

One of the tastiest northern salads is started by washing 4 cups of tender young rock cress and 2 cups of one of the blander greens. Dry thoroughly in a towel; then tear into bite sizes and mix in a large bowl. Prepare the dressing by shaking in a jar 1/2 cup of salad oil, 2 tablespoons wine vinegar, 2 tablespoons honey, a teaspoon salt, and 1/8 teaspoon pepper. Pour over the greens and toss diligently. Serve at once.

Rock cress also makes a better than usual wilted salad. Wash, dry thoroughly in a towel, tear into bite sizes, and drop into a salad bowl enough young rosettes for four. Starting with a cold frypan, sauté 4 slices of bacon over low heat, tilting the pan so that the grease will flow to one side and the bacon will become crisp. Remove the slices and tip the hot fat over the greens. Quickly heat a tablespoon of vinegar in the same pan. Pour this over the greens as well and toss until the leaves are thoroughly coated. Crumble the bacon over the top and serve immediately.

The radish-like taste of rock cress really touches up a soup. Wash 4 cups of some bland young greens, such as one of the wild lettuces, and 1/2 cup of rock cress rosettes, tearing all into bite sizes. Melt 3 tablespoons of butter or margarine in a large saucepan, add a small chopped onion, and sauté until tender. Add the greens, salt and pepper to taste, and cook over low heat until wilted. Then pour in a quart of poultry stock, made with bouillon cubes if necessary, and bring to a simmer.

Now mix 2 egg yolks with 1/2 cup of heavy cream. Add that. Stirring, heat only until a few bubbles are plopping lazily to the surface. Correct the seasonings. Place a buttered, crisply toasted slice of some substantial white bread, such as sourdough, in each of the quartet of soup plates. Pour the repast over them.

ABUNDANT AND SUBSTANTIAL INDIAN MAINSTAY

ACORNS

(Quercus)

THERE IS NO NEED FOR ANYONE to starve where acorns abound, and from 200 to 500 oaks (botanists differ) grow in the world. Some eighty-five of these are native to the United States. Although some of the latter species are scrubby, the genus includes some of our biggest and most stately trees. Furthermore, except in our northern prairies, oaks are widely distributed throughout the contiguous states, thriving at various altitudes and in numerous types of soil.

Abundant and substantial, acorns are perhaps this country's most important wildlife food. The relatively tiny acorns of the willow oak, pin oak, and water oak are often obtainable near streams and ponds, where they are relished by mallards, wood ducks, pintails, and other waterfowl. Quail devour such small acorns and peck the kernels out of the larger nuts.

Pheasants, grouse, pigeons, doves, and prairie chickens enjoy the nuts as well as the buds. Wild turkeys gulp down whole acorns regardless of their size. Squirrels and chipmunks are among the smaller animals storing acorns for off-season use. Black-tailed mule and white-tailed deer, elk, peccaries, and mountain sheep enjoy the acorns and also browse on twigs and foliage. Black bears grow fat on acorns.

Acorns probably rated the top position on the long list of wild foods depended on by the Indians. It has been stated, for example, that acorn soup, or mush, was the chief daily food of more than three-quarters of the native Californians. The eastern settlers were early introduced to acorns, too. In 1620 during their first hungry winter in Plymouth, the Pilgrims were fortunate enough to discover baskets of roasted acorns which the Indians had buried in the ground. In parts of Mexico and in Europe, the natives today still use acorns in the old ways.

All acorns are good to eat. Some are less sweet than others, that's all. But the bitterness that is prevalent in differing degrees is due to tannin, the same ingredient that causes tea to be bitter. Although it is not digestible in large amounts, it is soluble in water. Therefore, even the bitterest acorns can be made edible in an emergency.

Oaks comprise the most important group of hardwood timber trees on this continent. A major proportion of our eastern forests is oak. Its dense, durable wood has many commercial uses. Furthermore, oaks are among the most popular shade trees along our streets and about our dwellings.

The oaks may be separated into two great groups: the white oaks and the red oaks. The acorns of the former are the sweet ones. They mature in one growing season. The inner surfaces of the shells are smooth. The leaves typically have rounded lobes, but they are never bristle-tipped. The bark is ordinarily grayish and is generally scaly.

Among the red oaks, the usually bitter acorns do not mature until the end of the second growing season. The inner surfaces of the shells are customarily coated with woolly hair. The leaves have distinct bristles at their tips or at the tops of their lobes. The typically dark bark is ordinarily furrowed.

Indians used acorns both by themselves and in combination with other foods. For example, the Digger Indians roasted their acorns from the western white oak, *Quercus lobata,*

EASTERN WHITE OAK

hulled them, and ground them into a coarse meal which they formed into cakes and baked in crude ovens. In the East, the acorns of the white oak, *Quercus alba,* were also ground into meal but then were often mixed with the available cornmeal before being shaped into cakes and baked. Roasted and ground white oak acorns provide one of the wilderness coffees.

Indians leached their bitter acorns in a number of ways. Sometimes the acorns would be buried in swamp mud for a year, after which they would be ready for roasting and eating whole. Other tribes let their shelled acorns mold in baskets, then buried them in clean freshwater sand. When they had turned black, they were sweet and ready for use.

Some tribes ground their acorns by pounding them in stone pestles, many of which are found today, and then ran water through the meal by one method or another for often the greater part of a day until it was sweet. The meal might be placed in a specially woven basket for this purpose, or it might just be buried in the sandy bed of a stream.

To make the familiar, somewhat sweetish soup or gruel of the results, all that is necessary is to heat the meal in water. The Indians generally used no seasoning. As a matter of fact, until the white man came they ordinarily had no utensils but closely woven baskets. These were flammable, of course, and the heating had to be done by putting in rocks heated in campfires. Still showing how little one can get along with, the tribe then ate from common baskets, using their fingers.

It's an easy thing to leach acorns today. Just shell your nuts and boil them whole in a kettle of water, changing the liquid every time it becomes yellowish. You can shorten the time necessary for this to as little as a couple of hours, depending of course on the particular acorns, if you keep a teakettle of water always heating on the stove while this process is continuing. The acorns can then be dried in a slow oven, with the door left ajar, and either eaten as is or ground into coarse bits for use like any other nuts or into a fine meal.

To make acorn cakes, mix 2 cups of the meal with 1/2 teaspoon salt and 3/4 cup of water to form a stiff batter. This will be improved if you let it stand at room temperature for about an hour before turning it into the skillet.

Heat 3 tablespoons cooking oil in a large frypan until a test drop of water will sizzle. Drop the batter from a tablespoon, using a greased spatula to shape cakes a bit over 3 inches in diameter. Reduce the heat and tan the cakes slowly on each side. They are good either hot or cold.

For acorn pancakes for two, combine a cup of acorn meal and a cup of regular flour with 2 tablespoons sugar, 3 teaspoons double-action baking powder, and 1/2 teaspoon salt. Beat 2 eggs, 1 1/2 cups milk, and 2 tablespoons liquid shortening. Get your preferably heavy frypan or griddle hot, short of smoking temperature, and grease it sparingly with bacon.

When everything is ready to go, mix the whole business very briefly into a thin batter. Overmixing will make these tough. For this reason, a slightly lumpy batter is preferable to one that's beaten smooth. Turn each hotcake only once, when the flapjack starts showing small bubbles. The second side will take only half as long to cook. Serve steaming hot with butter or margarine and sugar, maple syrup, or one of the wild jellies.

We think of antibiotics as modern developments, but some of the Indian tribes used to let their acorn meal accumulate a mold. This was scraped off, kept in a damp place, and used to treat sores and inflammations.

BREAD FROM THE VERY ROCKS

ICELAND MOSS

(Cetraria)

ICELANDERS SAY THAT BY VIRTUE OF Iceland moss a munificent Heaven has provided them bread from the very rocks. In Iceland, northern Europe, and across the treeless top of Alaska and Canada, it has kept actual thousands from starving. In this country it grows across the northern states, down into New Jersey, Pennsylvania, and the high country of North Carolina.

Iceland moss, one of the edible lichens, consists of a fungus and an alga growing in close partnership. It is eaten by moose, deer, elk, and grouse to a certain extent. In the Arctic realms, however, it is one of the main foods of such widely ranging browsers as the reindeer and caribou. These primitive plants, incidentally, are pioneers when it comes to soil manufacture. The bitter organic acids that are characteristic of them assist in decomposing the very rocks on which many of them grow.

Iceland moss is a low, mosslike plant with a structure of branching stems in place of leaves. Forming tufts and tangled masses on the ground, it grows some two to four inches tall. Forking and branching freely, it is variously colored brown and grayish white to reddish.

From the odorless mats formed by this lichen arise numerous stalks, the majority of them being thin, flattened, and less

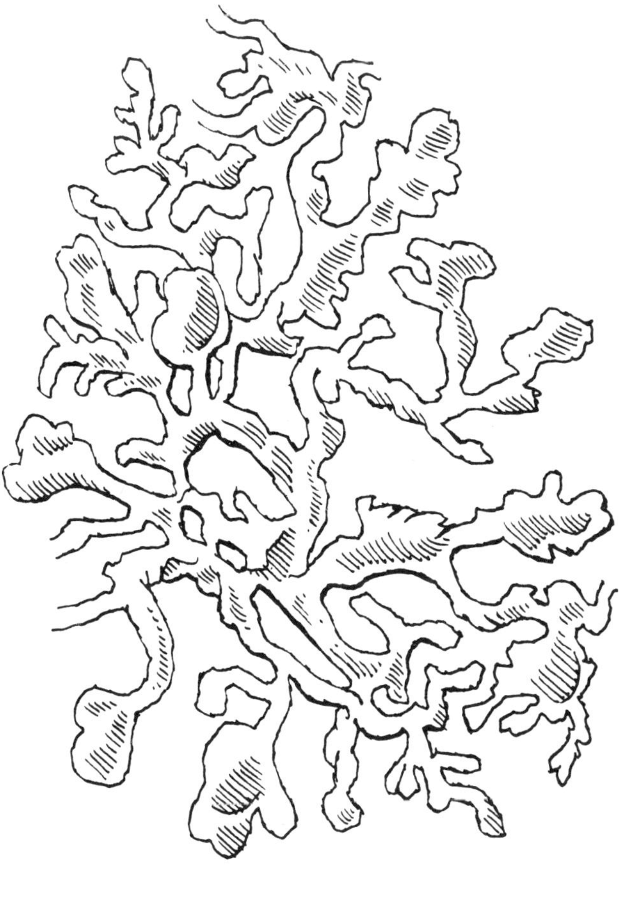

ICELAND MOSS

than one-tenth of an inch wide. The upper surfaces of these are generally smooth, the under expanses being paler, with wrinkles or channels toward the base. These stalks roll in at the edges, forming funnel-like tubes which terminate in flattened lobes with finely toothed edges. The spores, or fruits, when present grow mainly along the edges of the lobes.

Iceland moss has a marked rubbery texture during the summer. In winter the cold and the winds dehydrate the plants to brittleness. Upon soaking, they regain their rubbery characteristic.

Like most others, this lichen must be soaked before it is edible by humans. Otherwise, the unpleasantly bitter acids are apt to cause severe intestinal irritation. These acids can be removed easily enough, however, by soaking the Iceland moss in two changes of water, preferably with a teaspoon of baking soda added each time, then draining, drying, and finally crushing and pounding it to a powder. The result is so digestible that it is sold in some drugstores as a nutritive for invalids and convalescents.

When simmered with water or milk, this powder forms a jelly-like gruel, becoming firm upon cooling. The powder is added, too, to soups and stews. You can also use it, either as is or mixed half and half with wheat flour, to make cakes and bread.

Frying pan bread made with soaked and powdered Iceland moss is nutritious and substantial. Mix dry 2 cups of the powder, 2 teaspoons of baking powder, and 1/2 teaspoon of salt, taking all the time you need to do this thoroughly. Have your frypan warm and greased. Working quickly from now on, stir in enough cold water to make a firm dough. Shape this, with as little handling as possible, into a cake about an inch thick.

Lay the bannock in the warm frypan. Place it over low heat

until a bottom crust forms, rotating the pan a little so that the loaf will shift and not become stuck. Once the dough has hardened enough to hold together, you can turn the bannock over. This, if you've practiced a bit and have the confidence to flip strongly enough, can be easily accomplished with a slight swing of the arm and snap of the wrist. Or you can use a spatula or plate, supporting the loaf long enough to invert the frypan over it and then turning everything together. When a crust has formed all around, you may if you wish turn the bannock over a few more times while it is baking to an appetizing brown.

When is your Iceland moss bannock done? After you've been cooking them awhile, you will be able to tap one and gauge this by the hollowness of the sound. Meanwhile, test by shoving in a straw or toothpick. If any dough adheres, the loaf needs more heat. Cooking can be accomplished in about 15 minutes. The loaf should then be broken apart, never cut, and devoured piping hot, although cold bannock is good, too.

A SURVIVAL SUSTENANCE FOR LOVERS OF GOOD FOOD

SILVERWEED

(Potentilla)

THE BRIGHT GOLDEN BLOSSOMS OF SILVERWEED are common in damp places, haunting seacoast and stream banks, tarrying about stagnant ponds, and even shoving up amid salt meadow grasses. The white underneaths of the leaves are responsible for one of the common names of this edible. The roots, tasting like particularly good parsnips with overtones of sweet potato, have sometimes nourished people for months when other provisions were lacking.

Called argentine in French-speaking Canada, this food which grows in Europe and Asia as well as on this continent is also known as wild sweet potato, good tansy, wild tansy, cramp weed, and moor grass. It is luxuriant on the beaches and adjacent meadows of Alaska, where the natives and sourdoughs collect the fleshy roots in early spring as well as late fall, and extends over the roof of North America to Newfoundland. From there its range extends across the northern states, south along the Rocky Mountains to California and New Mexico.

Silverweed's relationship to the rose family is evinced by its lone, long-stemmed, five-petaled, inch-wide, bright yellow blossoms, which have the appearance of solitary roses. These

SILVERWEED

eventually produce fruit that make one think of dry strawberries. The leaves, all produced from the roots, are long and featherlike, being composed of many, stemless, oblong, toothed leaflets that are shining green above and silvery below.

The roots, which on this continent were Indian favorites, are the parts used, although ruffed grouse, woodcock, rabbit, and mountain sheep feast on the foliage. Good both raw and cooked, these roots are thick and fleshy.

The easiest way to prepare them is by roasting or boiling.

Candied, they are really special. For four, scrub about a pound of the roots. Simmer in a small amount of salted water until tender. Drain and slice. You'll need a stick of butter or margarine, 1/2 cup orange juice, 1/4 cup honey, 1/2 teaspoon grated orange rind, and 1/2 teaspoon salt. Place the silverweed, layer by layer, in a greased baking dish, flavoring each tier with dots of butter or margarine and some of the orange juice, honey, rind, and salt. Cover and bake in a moderate 350-degree oven for half an hour, carefully basting occasionally.

Silverweed patties are excellent, too, and can be quickly prepared in any amount. Just cook the scrubbed and sliced roots until tender in a minimum of salted water. Then mash and season with pepper, salt, and a liberal amount of butter or margarine. Shape in little cakes perhaps 2 1/2 inches broad. Dip in bread crumbs and sauté in butter or margarine until temptingly tanned on both sides.

These roots are also good with salt pork. Scrub and slice about a pound of the former, enough for four. Simmer, covered, in a small amount of salted water until tender. Then dice 1/2 pound of salt pork. Spread alternate layers of vegetables and meat in a greased casserole. Blend a tablespoon sugar, 1/2 teaspoon salt, and 1/8 teaspoon pepper, and sprinkle a little over each tier. Then pour 2/3 cup of beef broth over everything. Bake in a preheated moderate 350-degree oven for a half-hour and serve hot.

It is reasonable that so popular an edible as silverweed should have assumed a certain position in the medicine chest. The pioneers found silverweed tea efficacious in allaying diarrhea. This beverage was made by steeping a teaspoon of leaves in a cup of boiling water. It was drunk cold, one or two cupfuls a day, a few sips at a time.

A REGULAR FOOD CROP FOR THE TAKING

LAVER

(Porphyra)

ANYONE NEAR THE ATLANTIC OR PACIFIC shores of this continent seldom need worry about going without food in an emergency. Laver is one of the reasons.

Far from being just an emergency sustenance, though, this abundant seaweed furnishes a regular food crop in the Orient, and some has long been exported to this country. But exactly the same delicacy can be harvested here. And in a tight spot, it might even save your life.

Laver is the thin frond spied at low tide growing from rock ledges, boulders, and pier supports. You can see it wavering beneath the surface in still water, and heavy seas tear considerable quantities of it loose and toss it up on the shore. Very wavy edges characterize these long, narrow, sometimes leaflike seaweeds that grow up to about a foot long and from one to two inches wide. A second characteristic is the satiny gloss of these fronds with their filmy red, green, purple, and purplish brown elasticity.

Although laver is perfectly edible raw, it is better dried. In Alaska, for example, the natives gather it during the low tides of May and early June. It is separated from any foreign matter, then partially air- and sun-dried by being spread outdoors on fair days on a large cloth laid on the ground or on a table. It is chopped or ground in a food chopper, then again

LAVER

put out on sunny days, being repeatedly turned over and over until, blackening, it is thoroughly dried. Stored in closed containers in a dry, cool place, this dried laver can be kept indefinitely.

Dried laver is widely used in fish stews and soups, a cup to every 2 cups of liquid, after first being soaked for about an hour until tender. Too, it is commonly enjoyed raw, its crisp, salty taste being reminiscent of popcorn.

If you live close to the seacoast, a laver soup you can easily enjoy is started by simmering 2 cups of laver in a quart of water, stirring occasionally, until the water plant is tender. You can use fresh laver, or, for tastier results, dried laver that has been soaked an hour covered with fresh water, then drained.

In the meantime, slice a bunch of leeks very thinly almost to the root ends. Wash thoroughly, making sure all the grit is removed. Melt 2 tablespoons of butter or margarine in a preferably heavy frypan. Sauté the leeks in this until they are soft and just starting to tan. Add the boiling water with the laver, as well as a peeled and chopped tomato. Pepper to taste. Then boil rapidly for 10 minutes. Served with thin, hot toast, this is something most individuals want to repeat. Who says the best things in life aren't free?

WHO SAYS THE BEST THINGS IN LIFE AREN'T FREE?

WILD LETTUCE

(Lactuca)

A DELECTABLE AND VITAMIN-TEEMING RELATIVE of domesticated varieties, wild lettuce grows all the way across the continent from British Columbia to Newfoundland, south throughout the United States. About a dozen species of these tall, white-juiced edibles are common in the rich, moist soil of fields, yards, roadsides, and open thickets.

Ring-necked pheasants are among the birds feasting on the seeds. The prairie dog enjoys the foliage, while antelope and deer browse on the entire plants. Saddle and pack horses seem to find these delicately flavored greens particularly toothsome, too, even when they're too tough and old for the table.

Sometimes growing as high as a basketball player's reach, wild lettuce is hollow-stemmed and leafy. The generally smooth stalks have a whitish cast to them, as do the underneaths of the clasping stem leaves, which are abundant up to the loosely branched flower clusters. The deeply indented leaves growing from the base of the stalk become from several to twelve inches long. The numerous little narrow flowers range in color from bronze to yellow and blue.

If you like the slightly bitter taste of cooked dandelions, you'll enjoy wild lettuce as a potherb. Otherwise, discard the first water in which it is boiled. The leaves and stems are tender enough to cook until the edible is about sixteen inches high.

WILD LETTUCE

When just a few inches tall, wild lettuce makes a tasty salad. Green leafy vegetables as a whole deteriorate very quickly. Even when bought as fresh as obtainable from the best nearby store, they'll already have lost a large proportion of vitamins. Some of the food values of greens diminish as much as one-third the first hour after gathering. But pick them fresh from nature's own garden and eat them while they're at their tastiest, and you'll enjoy the best they have to offer, especially in the case of salad if you help things along by serving them on chilled plates.

For example, pick over, wash, and dry in a towel enough young wild lettuce for four. Tear into convenient pieces. Stirring, slowly pour the juice of a lemon into 1/2 cup of thick cream. Thoroughly mix in a teaspoon sugar, 1/4 teaspoon dry mustard, and 1/8 teaspoon paprika. Pour over the greens, season lightly to taste with salt, and toss. Serve immediately.

Bacon in particular brings out the taste of young wild lettuce. To go with 4 rather compactly filled cups of leaves that have been torn into bite-size portions in a salad bowl, start with a cold frypan and slowly cook 4 diced slices of bacon until crisp, tilting the fat to one side while the bits brown. Then add 1/4 cup cider vinegar, 2 teaspoons sugar, 1/2 teaspoon salt, and 1/8 teaspoon apiece of pepper, dry mustard, and paprika. Stir until well blended, pour hot over the greens, toss thoroughly, and serve.

Wild lettuce goes well with water cress, considered at length in *Free for the Eating.* Tear enough young wild lettuce for four into bite sizes and mix with 1/2 cup of chopped water cress. Toss with a dressing made by dissolving 1/4 teaspoon of salt in 2 tablespoons tarragon vinegar, adding 1/8 teaspoon pepper and the merest pinch of curry powder, and then whipping in 6 tablespoons of salad oil. Top with tiny pieces of white toast, well covered with garlic spread concocted by softening 1/2 stick of butter or margarine, then beating in with a fork a chopped clove of garlic and salt and pepper to taste. What spread you don't use on the spot can be kept covered in the refrigerator.

When wild lettuce is a little older, you'll prefer it cooked. Depending on the size, it is often possible to lift this green directly from the rinse to the saucepan and heat it without added water. If this edible is no longer quite young, add 2 tablespoons of boiling water. In either event, cover and cook over high heat only until tender. Then drain if necessary. The following four recipes are particularly effective with wild lettuce, torn into bite-size pieces and cooked this way. Each, like most of the recipes in this book, is geared to four people.

For the first, season the hot greens to taste with salt and pepper. Mix in 1/2 cup each of cubed cooked ham and hot croutons, freshly browned in butter or margarine. Serve immediately.

For the second, bring 1/2 cup of sour cream, along with a tablespoon of butter or margarine, to a bubble in a separate saucepan. Season to taste with salt and pepper. Add the hot greens, cook over low heat until bubbles again begin plopping to the surface, and serve hot.

For the third, drench the hot greens with a cup of preferably heavy cream. Add 3 tablespoons of butter or margarine. Sprinkle on salt and pepper to taste. Simmer for 5 minutes. Then rapidly stir in an egg yolk. Serve at once, garnished with the paprika-brightened slices of 4 hard-cooked eggs.

For the fourth, be sautéing a medium-size onion in a stick of butter or margarine until the bits are tan and tender. Add the hot greens and 2 cups of cooked rice, preferably wild. Mix well and get steaming hot. Season to taste with salt and pepper. Sprinkle with paprika, dust sparingly with nutmeg, and serve hot.

Cream of wild lettuce soup is well worth the making. You'll need 1 1/2 cups of cooked, well-drained greens for this recipe. Chop them and either press them through a sieve or puree them in the blender. Add them, along with a cup of milk and a teaspoon of grated onion, to a sauce made by melting 3 tablespoons of butter or margarine in a saucepan over moderate heat and blending 3 tablespoons of flour with it. Stirring hard, add 3 cups of hot milk and bring to a bubble. Stir in a well-beaten egg yolk, season to taste with salt and pepper, simmer 3 minutes, and serve.

Or turn 1 1/2 cups of cooked, drained, and chopped wild lettuce into a loaf that will be a delight to both eye and palate. Sauté a medium-size, finely chopped onion until golden in 1/2 stick of butter or margarine over low heat. Mix 1/4 cup of flour to a paste with a minimum of cold milk. Blend this smoothly with the remainder of 1 1/2 cups of milk. Stir into the onions and, continuing to stir, bring to a simmer, whereupon everything will thicken. Mix with the greens.

Beat 3 egg yolks with a teaspoon salt, 1/4 teaspoon black pepper, and 1/8 teaspoon rosemary. Add to the greens mixture. Then beat the 3 whites until they are stiff and fold them in. Smooth out in a pan measuring about 8 by 4 inches.

Get 3/4 of a cup of fresh crumbs, perhaps by cutting the crusts from soft white bread, tearing the remainder into small pieces, and feeding these a bit at a time into your electric blender. Stir the crumbs and 2 tablespoons of grated Parmesan cheese with a tablespoon of melted butter or margarine. Then sprinkle over the top of the loaf.

Bake in a preheated moderate 350-degree oven about an hour or until a knife inserted in the middle comes out clean. Allow to cool and firm for 15 minutes. Then invert on a hot platter, cut into half-inch slices, and serve.

THE CANDY COUNTER OF THE SWAMPS

SWEET FLAG

(Acorus)

CANDIED SWEET FLAG HAS SOMEWHAT THE same aromatic pungency as the now difficult-to-obtain candied ginger. To make your own, cut the tender bases of the stalks into very thin slices. Parboil in several changes of water to moderate the strong taste.

Then simmer, stirring frequently, barely covered with a syrup composed proportionately of 2 cups of sugar to every cup of water until most of the sugar has been absorbed. Drain, dry apart from one another on waxed paper or foil for several days, roll in granulated sugar, and pack what you don't devour on the spot in tightly closing jars.

The fleshy rootstalks were often used for this purpose in the days of wood fires, but they usually need to be kept on the back of a warm stove for several days to become sufficiently tender.

Sweet flag, a cousin of our friend the jack-in-the-pulpit, which also belongs to the arum family, grows in a wide band throughout southern Canada and the contiguous states, as well as in Europe and Asia. You see broad stands of it in marshes, swamps, damp grasslands, and along stagnant waters, where it is also known as calamus, myrtle flag, sweet rush, and sweet grass. The latter two names were inspired not only by the flavor of the stalk's interior but by the pleasantly aromatic fragrance of the bruised foliage. This was a

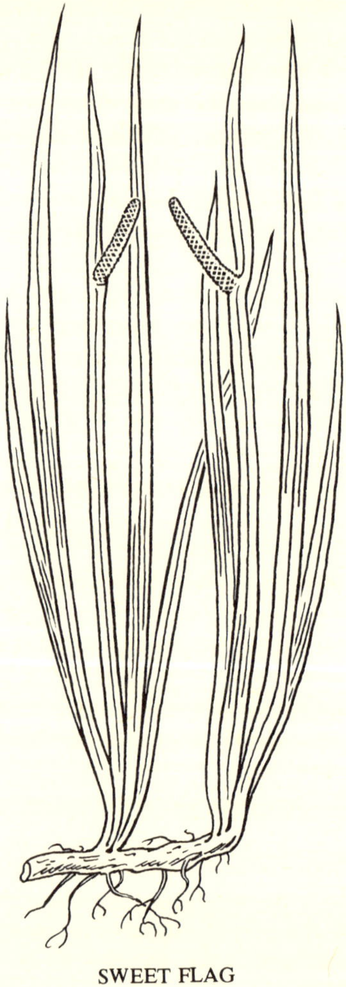

SWEET FLAG

major reason why our pioneer ancestors often chose these leaves to spread cleanly on the floors of their cabins.

This aroma is one characteristic that distinguishes the edible from the blue flag, the state flower of Tennessee. Also, the sweet flag has glossy, yellowish green leaves, whereas those of the blue flag are both dull and bluish green. There is also the spicy pungency of the sweet flag's rootstock, a little of which is sometimes eaten raw as a remedy for indigestion.

Or you can make a tea from the roots, which can be dried and grated for the purpose. Stored in a tightly closed jar, these roots will keep for months. The recommended dosage is a teaspoonful to a cup of boiling water, drunk cold one or two cupfuls a day, several sips at a time. You may prefer this sweetened. In pioneer days it was held to be a remedy for sour or upset stomach, as well as a general stimulant to digestion.

The sharp, thin, swordlike leaves of the sweet flag grow up to about four feet tall. They sheathe one another tightly at the base, often beneath the surface of the ground or mud. Stout, horizontal roots with their unmistakable gingery taste spread from them in closely intertwined mats.

The flower stalk grows almost as tall as the leaves. About halfway up it the spikelike spadix, several inches long and reminiscent of the "jack" of the jack-in-the-pulpit, grows off on an angle. This becomes closely covered with tiny yellowish green flowers.

Raw sweet flag offers prime emergency food in the spring, when the partially grown flower stalks are edible and when the interiors of the young stalks, crammed with half-formed leaves, are sweet and tasty enough to be taken home for salads.

THE SHRUB THAT AFFORDS BOTH FRUIT AND JEWELRY

BARBERRY

(Berberis)

DEPENDING ON WHICH BOTANIST IS DOING the defining, there are some fifteen species of barberry in this country. These shrubs, common along many a road, generally grow in well-drained upland areas. Deer eat them, despite the thorns of some, and so do elk and mountain sheep. Rabbits and their cousins, the varying hares, nibble on bark, leaves, and twigs. Ruffed grouse and ring-necked pheasants are among the birds devouring the berries.

Barberries, which grow from one coast to the other, become fragrant masses of yellow flowers in the spring, glossy rich green expanses in the summer, and brilliant crimsons and bronzes during the crisp weather of autumn. Berries range from orangy and scarlet to the fine blue of the so-called Oregon grape. In the Southwest, you can sometimes find at little roadside shops neck crosses simply made of the distinctively beautiful yellow wood of the barberry.

The leaves of the *Berberis vulgaris*, a typical barberry shrub, grow, often in clusters, on slender, curved gray branches. Ranging from about an inch to an inch and a half long, they are rounded at their tops and narrowing at the bases. They have stiff, coarse hairs and are toothed around the edges. Triple-tipped spines appear in place of leaves on some of the younger shoots. The quarter-inch flowers,

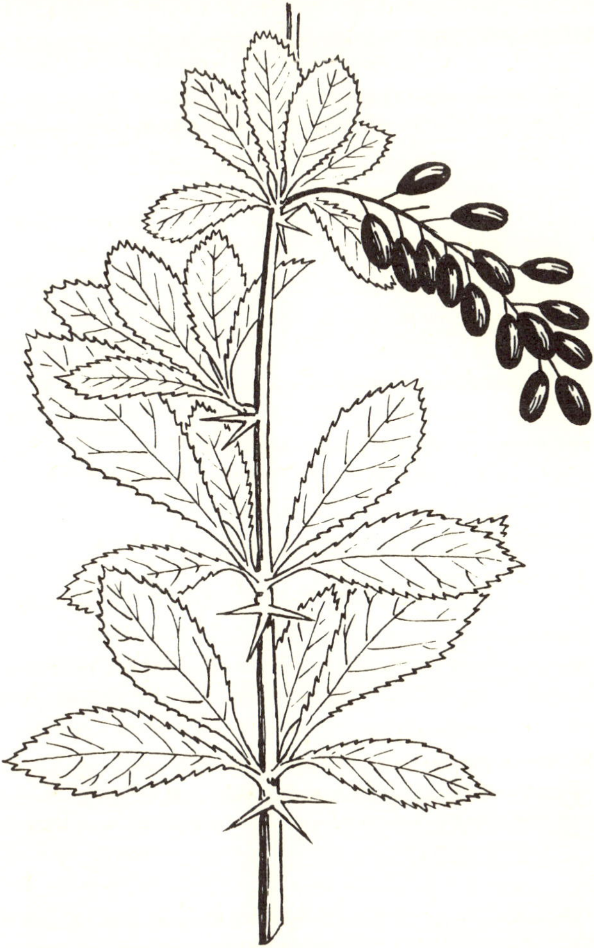

BARBERRY

growing in drooping, elongated clusters like those of the lily of the valley, give way to dense, acid fruit.

Both the Indians and the early settlers dried the fruit for winter use, made an agreeably cooling drink from it, and turned much of it into pleasantly tart sauces and preserves. The jelly closely rivals that of the highbush cranberry (see *Free for the Eating*), which to many palates is the best made. Too, housewives used to add the berries to sweeter, blander fruits to give them character.

The tough, hard roots of the barberry were crushed and boiled to make a bright yellow dye for baskets, fabrics, and buckskins. The stems and bark were also sometimes used for this purpose. The Karok Indians pounded the blue fruit of the Oregon grape with other ingredients to make a paint for embellishing their bows and arrows.

The bitter root of the barberry was also used as a tonic and laxative. One of the earlier purgatives on this continent was a teaspoonful of the powdered bark of the root in a glass of water. Taken in small amounts during the day, this concoction was also held to be a tonic and blood purifier. Externally, it was employed as a lotion to treat various skin diseases.

The Indians used to chew the root and use the resulting liquid for wounds. The roots are too bitter for many who nevertheless find that chewing a couple of the pleasantly acid leaves is refreshing when they're thirsty and no water is handy. The Indians used to steep these leaves and drink the tea for rheumatism.

You can make straight barberry jelly, extracting the juice from the cooked berries with the help of a jelly bag and then boiling it until it runs from the tip of a spoon in a sheet or your jelly thermometer reads 220 to 222 degrees. This jelly requires no pectin.

Years when the barberry crop is sparse, you may have to add water to the berries when first softening them by cooking. Then if you add apples to make the extraction jell, you may like the results even better. Today, where used, barberry-apple jelly is one of the favorites with game.

To make it, pick over and wash 4 cups of wild barberries. Quarter 4 tart apples, leaving cores and skins but removing the stems and blossom ends. Simmer the berries and apples, along with 3 cups of water, until everything is soft. Then move to a jelly bag. If you do not squeeze this, you'll have a clearer, more sparkling jelly. By the way, if you want the basis for some refreshing drinks in the summertime, just bottle this barberry juice as is for use later with sugar and ice.

Otherwise, bring the juice to a boil, stir in an equal volume of sugar, and heat until 2 drops will come together on the edge of a metal spoon and run off in a sheet, or until your jelly thermometer reads 220 to 222 degrees. Pour into hot, sterile glasses that have been set on a towel, away from drafts. Fill to within 1/4 inch of the top. Pour a thin layer of melted paraffin over the top, tipping each glass slightly so that this will adhere to all the edges. Cool, add a second thin layer of wax, cover with a lid or foil, and store in a cool, dry place.

You can also make a rich sauce by combining equal volumes of barberries and molasses, simmering this until the fruit is soft. Then run everything through a sieve to remove the fruit, boil the liquid until about half of it has evaporated, tip in the fruit, bring everything to a boil, and finally pour it into hot, sterilized glasses. Seal these as above.

To go with cold venison sandwiches, there's nothing like cold barberry tarts. For the pastry, cut 1 1/2 cups shortening into 2 cups all-purpose flour until it is the consistency of large peas. Then add a bit at a time enough cold water, about 1/3 cup, to make your dough. Shape this into a ball, wrap in foil or waxed paper or place in a covered bowl, and chill overnight in the refrigerator. When ready to go, roll out 1/8-inch thick and cut into 3-inch squares.

Make your filling by simmering 3 cups of barberries with 1 1/2 cups sugar and 1/3 cup water until the fruit mashes easily. Then press through a strainer. Place a tablespoon of the puree on each square of pastry. Fold together to make a triangle, moisten the edges with cold water, and press together with a fork. Preheat the oven to a hot 425 degrees and bake 25 minutes or until the tarts are a rich brown.

A DELICATELY FLAVORED WEED, SO RICH IN NOURISHMENT

GREEN AMARANTH

(Amaranthus)

PLANTS MANUFACTURE THEIR OWN VITAMINS, AND the nutritious green amaranth is rich in minerals as well. In addition, it is one of the most delicious of the greens, wild or otherwise. The tender tops, stalks, and leaves of this wild spinach, which has none of the strong taste of market varieties, are delightfully esculent from early spring to frost-blighting fall.

Growing as a weed over much of the continent including the tropics, the green amaranth is familiar to most individuals, although not necessarily as an edible. The stout, rough stalks, usually unbranched, sometimes reach the height of a man, but small, tender plants can usually be found growing in the same patch. These stems are slightly hairy.

The dull green leaves are long-pointed ovals with wavy edges. Their stems, also edible, are nearly as long as they are themselves. The roots, the reason for the occasional name of redroot and wild beet, are attractively red. Another name is pigweed, applied because the green amaranth prefers rich soil such as that found around pigpens and barns.

The flowers are greenish and, being such, are usually not recognized as blossoms. They grow in long, loosely branched clusters. Exuding the faint, evocative scent of spring, they have a pleasant taste raw. The resulting shiny black seeds were threshed by the Indians, roasted, and then used for cakes and porridge. Some outdoorsmen like to scatter a handful atop a bannock before consigning this frying pan bread to the heat.

The extremely delicate flavor of green amaranth is something many prefer to that of almost any other green. This fragility of taste lends itself to a wide range of cooking procedures. You can also influence the final results by including some less bland vegetable, such as water cress.

But at least try some just started in a minimum of boiled salted water and cooked, covered, as briefly and as rapidly as possible. Young green amaranth can be lifted directly from rinse to saucepan, salted sparingly, and cooked without additional fluid. Serve with just margarine or butter melting yellowly over the top.

Young green amaranth is also notable raw. Wash, dry, and tear into bite-size pieces enough tender greens for four. Toast 4 slices of white bread, rub both sides with a halved clove of garlic, cut into small cubes, and sauté until golden in butter or margarine. Season the greens to taste with salt and pepper, add the croutons, a cup of French dressing, 4 tablespoons crumbled Roquefort cheese, toss thoroughly, and serve.

Or for another highly pleasing dinner salad, prepare the dressing sometime during the afternoon by mixing in the bottom of your salad bowl a minced clove of garlic, 1/2 cup of salad oil, 2 tablespoons wine vinegar, 2 teaspoons chopped water cress, 1/4 teaspoon black pepper, and salt to taste. Leave at room temperature, stirring occasionally. Just before the meal, toss with enough washed, towel-dried, and shredded greens for four.

Wilted green amaranth is also excellent. Tear 4 loosely

GREEN AMARANTH

packed cups of washed and well-dried young greens into bite-sized segments. Put into a bowl that has been freshly rubbed with a halved clove of garlic. Sauté 4 chopped slices of bacon over low heat until crisp, starting with a cold frypan and tilting it so that the grease will run to one side. Add 6 tablespoons salad oil, 2 tablespoons tarragon vinegar, 1/4 teaspoon celery salt, and 1/8 teaspoon of preferably freshly ground black pepper. Bring to a simmer, pour over the amaranth, cover with a plate, and allow to steam 5 minutes. Then toss and serve on warm dishes.

Here's another version that adds even more flavor to these bland greens. Wash, dry, and shred 4 cups of loosely packed amaranth. Heap in a salad bowl and sprinkle with 1/4 teaspoon salt. Mix in a teaspoon of chopped water cress and 1/2 teaspoon grated onion. Chop 4 slices of bacon and sauté this until the bits are crisp and golden. Add 1/2 cup wine vinegar and a teaspoon of sugar to the bacon grease and bring to a bubble for 3 minutes.

You now have your choice. You may turn the hot sauce over the raw greens and blend well. Or you may tip the greens into the frypan and cook over low heat until they are limp. In either event, serve immediately, garnished with the bacon bits and 2 sliced, hard-cooked eggs.

There's a pristine delicacy to creamed green amaranth. Simmer enough whole greens for four in a very small amount of salted water. While they are seething, tightly covered, prepare your sauce by melting 2 tablespoons of butter or margarine in a pan over heat so low that the grease doesn't color. Then smoothly stir in an equal volume of flour. Be bringing a cup of milk to a simmer. Stirring to prevent lumping, add this. Bring to a bubble, whereupon it will thicken. Keep bubbling for 5 minutes, seasoning to taste with salt and pepper and with 1/8 teaspoon nutmeg. As soon as the greens are tender, drain them, chop them, and blend them with the steaming sauce. Serve immediately.

Green amaranth cream soup will enhance the finest dinner. For enough for four, you'll need 2 cups of pureed green amaranth, made by cooking the wild vegetable until soft and then reducing it to a pulp by putting it through a sieve or the blender. Warm this with a quart of milk.

In the bottom of a saucepan, melt 3 tablespoons of butter or margarine. Blend 2 teaspoons of cornstarch with this, not letting either brown. Gradually stir in the puree and milk. Season to taste with salt and pepper. Heat at no more than a simmer until the soup thickens slightly. Then stir in 2 eggs that have been beaten with 1/2 cup of cream, warm a minute more, and ladle out.

Feel like a little well-spent effort? To go with 2 cups of cooked green amaranth, drained thoroughly and then either put through a colander or such or pureed in the blender, sauté 1 1/2 tablespoons of finely minced onion in 1/2 stick of butter or margarine in a large frypan until well tanned. Smoothly blend in 4 tablespoons of flour. Then, stirring until everything thickens, slowly add a cup of light cream.

Turning the heat to low, beat 4 egg yolks until frothy. Stir in a bit of the hot mixture from the frypan. Then turn the yolks into the pan, mix in a cup of white bread crumbs, and, stirring, cook 2 minutes. Add the greens and heat. Season to taste with about a teaspoon of salt and 1/4 teaspoon of pepper.

Take off the heat. Beat the 4 egg whites until they are stiff and fold them into the mixture. Pour into a well-greased ring mold. Set this in a pan of boiling water. Bake in a preheated moderate 325-degree oven for about a half-hour or until a knife inserted in the mousse comes out dry. Then turn upside down on a hot platter, fill the center with creamed young carrots, and serve at once.

Then there are green amaranth molds that some always enjoy at least once each spring. To go with 1 1/2 cups of cooked amaranth, well drained and chopped fine, add a cup of milk and heat to a bubble only. Beat until frothy 4 eggs, a teaspoon salt, 1/2 teaspoon lemon juice, and 1/8 teaspoon pepper. Mix in a bit of the greens. Then stir into the greens and milk. Bring again to a bubble.

Turn the simmering mixture into 4 well-greased cups or molds. Set these in a pan, pour boiling water around them, and bake in a preheated moderate 350-degree oven for about a half-hour or until a knife inserted into one of the centers comes out dry. Turn onto hot plates and eat immediately.

You can have a fine one-dish meal with green amaranth, too. Get things going by placing 8 eggs, one by one with a spoon, in enough boiling water to cover them by an inch. Let the temperature immediately drop to a simmer and keep it that way for 10 minutes. Then remove the eggs from the heat and plunge them into cold water. If the shells are cracked slightly before the eggs cool, peeling will be easier. Slice the eggs carefully.

In the meantime, be simmering enough green amaranth in a minimum of salted water to fill 2 cups when drained. Cook, covered, only until a test piece, still slightly crisp, proves soft enough to eat.

You'll need to prepare your sauce, too. Melt 6 tablespoons of butter or margarine in a pan over moderate heat, not letting it brown. Stir in 6 tablespoons of flour until it is well blended. Still stirring, pour in 2 cups of milk that has been brought to a bubble in another pan. Season to taste with salt and pepper and with 1/8 teaspoon of mace. As soon as this sauce comes to a simmer, it will thicken. Then stir in 1 1/2 cups of grated Cheddar cheese bit by bit, lower the heat, and continue stirring until the cheese has smoothly melted.

Spread a portion of the greens over the bottom of a greased casserole. Top this with a roofing of chopped eggs. Keep on doing this until the green amaranth and the eggs are all gone, ending with the vegetable. Pour the cheese sauce over everything, sprinkle with paprika, and bake in a moderate 350-degree oven for half an hour. Like most of the recipes in the book, this will serve four.

THE DELECTABLE ROOTS THAT TASTE LIKE SHELLFISH

SALSIFY

(Tragopogon)

THE THREE SPECIES OF SALSIFY THAT thrive from coast to coast in this country and in southern Canada are also known as goatsbeard and as oyster plant. The last name takes note of salsify's similarity in taste, to some palates, to that of the shellfish. To others, however, the roots have more the pleasant flavor of parsnips. The only secret is to get these roots while they are tender. The tops are used, too, both for salads and for cooked greens.

In many localities salsify is common along roadsides and in fields. Often growing two and three feet high, salsify is a tall perennial with a primary root that extends vertically downward. This becomes too pithy for use once the tall, leafy flowering stem develops the second year, producing either yellow or purple blooms not unlike large dandelion blossoms.

Also like dandelions, the leaves exude a milky juice when scraped or broken. They resemble wide blades of grass. Salsify is so good that the roots are grown commercially both on this continent and in Europe, the only difference between them and the wild variety being that the latter are usually smaller.

Salsify roots can be a treat. Scrub them. Then scrape them. If you are preparing them beforehand, keep them in cold water along with a tablespoon of vinegar to prevent their

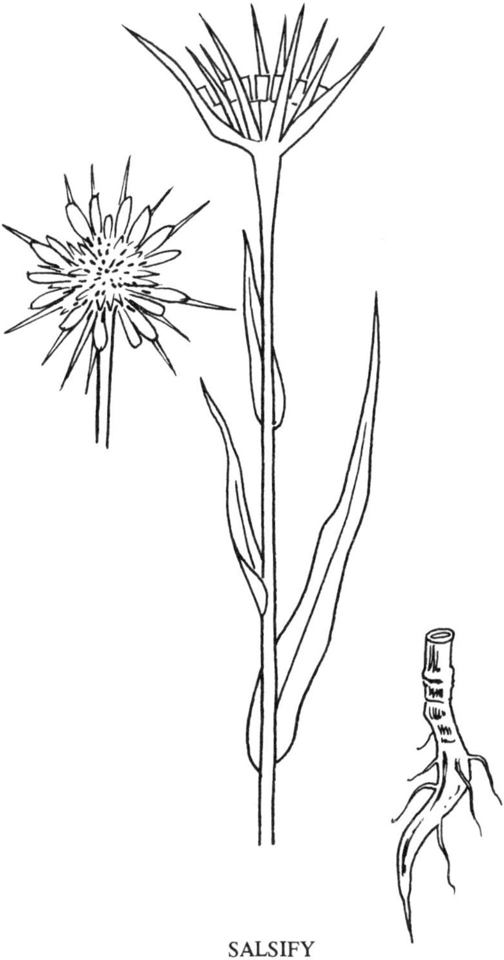

SALSIFY

discoloring. When ready to use, cut into half-inch slices. Bring to a simmer in lightly salted water, in a covered saucepan, and cook until a table fork will easily penetrate the center of a test slab. Drain, salt and pepper to taste, and serve with melting butter or margarine.

Salsify cooked this way is also tasty with white sauce. A good one for this purpose can be made by melting 2 tablespoons of butter or margarine in a saucepan over moderate heat. Sauté 2 slices of onion briefly in this without letting either the grease or the vegetable brown. Then blend in 2 tablespoons of flour. Still stirring, slowly add a cup of milk and simmer for 5 minutes. Season to taste with salt and pepper. Then strain and serve. Incidentally, cold boiled salsify can be reheated in such a sauce.

Cold boiled salsify can also be very satisfactorily sautéed in a liberal amount of butter, margarine, or salad oil. Turn the pieces until they are well browned on both sides. Then season them with salt and pepper. If you prefer, first roll them well in seasoned flour instead of salting and peppering them later.

Sometime when you're having another couple over for dinner and really want to show them what can be accomplished with a wild vegetable, dice 2 cups of scrubbed and scraped salsify. Drop the bits, along with a cup of light cream, into the top of a double boiler over boiling water. Season with salt and, in this case particularly, preferably with freshly ground black pepper. This salsify, stirred about every 15 minutes, will take about 2 hours to become tender. Keep hot until ready to serve.

French-fried salsify goes well with steak. Scrub and scrape enough roots for four. Then cut each lengthwise as you would potatoes. Simmer in salted water until nearly tender. Drain and chill.

In the meantime, beat 2 eggs with 1/2 cup of light cream. Season a cup of flour with salt and pepper. Dredge the salsify in the flour. Dip in the liquid. Then roll in white bread crumbs, pressing on all that you can. Melt 2 sticks of butter or margarine in a shallow frypan. As soon as it starts to color, put in the salsify so that each piece is separate. Fry, turning, until golden. Serve sizzling.

Salsify is also good sugared. Again scrub, scrape, and slice lengthwise enough of the roots for four. Simmer in salted water until nearly tender. In the meantime, mix a tablespoon of sugar with 1/4 teaspoon of salt and 1/8 teaspoons each of cinnamon, pepper, nutmeg, and mace. Melt a stick of butter or margarine. Have 1/4 cup of flour ready. Roll each piece in the sugar mixture. Then dip into the fat. Dredge with flour. Sprinkle with sugar. Fry in 2 sticks of butter or margarine, turning until golden.

The leaves are well worth eating when you catch them young. Wash a quart of greens, dry them thoroughly with a towel, tear into bite-size segments, and pile in a salad bowl that has been rubbed with a halved clove of garlic.

Fry 4 diced slices of bacon, starting as always with a cold frypan and tilting the accumulating grease to one side. When the bits are brown, remove them. Add to the frypan 1/2 cup cider vinegar, a teaspoon sugar, a teaspoon diced onion, 1/2 teaspoon salt, and 1/8 teaspoon pepper. Simmer over low heat for 3 minutes. Then pour over the greens and toss thoroughly. Garnish with the bacon, 2 sliced hard-cooked eggs, and a tablespoon of chopped water cress. Serve immediately.

VALUABLE BERRIES THAT ASSURE BOTH FOOD AND LIGHT

BAYBERRIES

(Myrica)

THE SHINY EVERGREEN LEAVES OF THE bayberry, used in moderation and removed before the dish is brought to the table, will do wonderful things for soups, stew, broths, and steaming chowders. As for the greenish berries, which ripen to white, they have been valued since Colonial days for making soaps and scenting candles.

The bayberry—also called wax myrtle, candleberry, wax-berry, and a horde of local names—is essentially a seaboard small tree and stocky shrub, although it follows the broad St. Lawrence River inland to the start of the Great Lakes. Seven species are native to this country and southern Canada, one along the Pacific Coast and the other six in the East. Too, bayberries are widely planted as a part of landscape gardening.

Numerous varieties of birds consume the picturesque berries. These include duck, grouse, turkey, and the scurrying quail. Incidentally, the fruit should not be given to pen-raised quail, as its waxiness interferes with their digestion. Foxes also devour the berries, while deer browse on the twigs and foliage.

The bark of these evergreen shrubs and small trees, with their characteristically stiff branches, is gray. The narrowly oblong leaves, from one to four inches long, are occasionally slightly toothed. The attractive fruit, actually a nutlet, is based on a hard stone that encloses a two-seeded kernel. On the outside of the stone are gunpowder-like grains. Over these is a dryish, pleasantly scented crust of granular, greenish-white wax that once smelled will never be forgotten. The leaves, too, when bruised, give off a memorable aroma.

If bayberries grow near your home, you may choose to pick two or three leaves whenever you're cooking a stew or such. The leaves can also be satisfactorily preserved. Just gather the shiniest and greenest of them, perhaps during that summer or early autumn vacation at the seashore, and bring them home in a bag. Then spread them out and dry them in the kitchen or attic. Pack them in tightly closing jars. Store them in a dark cabinet where they'll be handy. They're apt to become one of your favorite spices.

Growing as it does from Newfoundland to Florida, the bayberry was one of the earliest American plants used for medicine by the settlers venturing up and down the eastern seaboard of the New World. The dried bark of the root, preferably gathered just before winter, was pounded into powder and stored, tightly enclosed, in a dark place. A teaspoonful to a cup of boiling water, drunk cold one or two cupfuls a day, was used to quiet diarrhea. Pioneers also sniffed this powder with reportedly good effect for catarrh and nasal congestion. It was also occasionally applied in poultices to cuts and inflammations.

Some stores feature bayberry candles and soap, but you'll enjoy these even more if you make them yourself. First, you'll need a lot of bayberries. Free these of twigs and leaves and, by washing them a few at a time in a colander, of all dust. Put them in a large kettle filled with water and heat them very slowly so that as the sediment floats to the top, where it should be removed, it will not cook into the wax. Then set everything aside to cool. Left in the cold for several hours, the wax will form a hard cake.

Take this out and remove as much of the adhering dirt as you can. Then put the cake into a smaller kettle filled with fresh water and set it again over low heat. Once the wax has remelted, run everything through a strainer and then through cheesecloth. Do this in the warm kitchen, but then set the mixture in the cold once more. If the rehardening wax does not seem clean enough, go through the whole procedure again. The block of wax you have left can be melted for making tapers or soap.

It takes ten pounds of bayberries to give a pound of wax. This, in turn, will supply two substantial candles. The housewives of yore had plenty of time, but even today the work is satisfying. And what makes better Christmas gifts?

The art of dipping candles is an ancient one. Today you'll be best advised, though, to buy your wicks, perhaps in a hobby shop. You can also purchase molds, for that matter, although there is something particularly eye-catching about the gratifying roughness of candles you dip by hand.

Just melt your wax in a deep container, perhaps a clean tall can you have reserved for the purpose. Start by tying some weight, if only a pebble, to the bottom of the wick, so as to straighten it out as you immerse it in the wax that is just warm enough to remain in the melted state. Once your taper has been started, you can cut off this weight so as to have a flat base.

As soon as each layer of wax has cooled, dip the candle again. Tying the tops of the wicks apart from one another on a short stick, you can be dipping two or three candles at once. When they have built up nearly to the desired size, shave

BAYBERRY

them a bit perhaps with a knife. Then the final dip or two will give them the desired rugged slickness.

Pioneers used hollow lengths of cane and carefully rolled cylinders of birch bark for their molds, and you can do the same thing. Start by suspending the wick from a short stick laid across the top of the upright mold. Then fill the latter with the odoriferous bayberry wax, perhaps pouring this handily from an old teapot.

Fasten the mold so that it will remain undisturbed in an upright position for half a day in the cold. Then, loosening the base with a sharp knife, pull it out by the cross stick. If it does not slide readily, the trouble may be that your wax was not clean enough. All you'll have to do, though, is run hot water over the mold. Then once the candle is loose, hold it upright until it is firm enough to lay down.

Some use bayberry soap the year around. In making this, use enamel, iron, or earthenware utensils. Do not employ aluminum. Avoid fumes and watch out you do not splash lye on your hands. If lye is spilled, rinse the object with weak vinegar. Lye becomes very hot and may break a glass container.

For 9 pounds of soap, use:

6 pounds bayberry wax
1/4 cup borax (optional)
1 can lye (3 ounces)
2 1/2 pints soft water

For 1 bar of soap, use:

1 cup bayberry wax
1 teaspoon borax (optional)
5 teaspoons lye
1/2 cup soft water

Dissolve the lye in soft water a little at a time. Use rain water, snow water, or melted ice. If no soft water is available, "break" hard water by adding 1 to 2 tablespoons of lye to a gallon. Let stand overnight and then remove the scum. Bring this solution to a lukewarm 85 degrees.

Melt your wax and then cool it to 110 degrees, slightly warmer than body heat. Add the borax to the melted wax and stir. This will improve the sudsing action of the soap.

Add the lye solution to the wax in a steady, thin stream. Stir evenly and slowly. If you stir too fast, the soap will curdle and not combine. Continue mixing in this fashion for 10 to 20 minutes or until the solution is like thin honey. A greasy layer indicates it is too warm. Then put the kettle in cool water and stir from sides and bottom. If it is lumpy, it is too cold. Put it in a pan of hot water. Within a half-hour, the mixture should thicken.

Pour the thickened mixture into a mold. For a mold, use a flat enameled pan or a wood or cardboard box lined with wet cotton cloth. Cover with a heavy rug or blanket for a day and a night, depending on where you live, as freezing will spoil the soap. Cut into bars of desired size with a string. Stack these bars in an airy place and age them for two weeks before you use any.

If this soap separates, or is crumbly or greasy, reclaim it by boiling in a large kettle. Add 7 pints of soft water to the large recipe or 1 cup of soft water to the small recipe. Dissolve the soap slowly. Then increase heat and boil until it thickens. Since it boils over readily, select a large kettle and stir constantly. Then pour into the mold as above.

THE FAMOUS VEGETABLE THAT HELPED THE SIOUX DEFEAT CUSTER

PRAIRIE TURNIP

(Psoralea)

WHEN JOHN COLTER, A MOUNTAIN MAN once with the Lewis and Clark expedition, escaped from the Indians and came back safely with his incredible story of what now is Yellowstone National Park, he lived for a week largely on prairie turnips. This famous vegetable of the plains and the West, a mainstay of such Indians as the Sioux, is also known as the prairie apple, Indian breadroot, wild potato, *pomme blanche, pomme de prairie,* and wild turnip. Early plainsmen, frontiersmen, settlers, trappers, traders, and explorers soon came to relish its starchy, sweetish, and somewhat turnip-like taste.

The prairie turnip is a member of the pea family. It is a perennial whose large root, or sometimes group of roots, resembling sweet potato roots, lies entirely beneath the ground. The generally branched stalks, characterized by soft, whitish bristles, are erect and from about six to eighteen inches tall. Five inversely ovate leaflets, narrowest at their bases, comprise each leaf. These leaflets are about one-half to an inch wide and twice as long. The plant blooms with dense spikes of small, bluish, pealike flowers which eventually become tiny pods.

The tops of the prairie turnips mature early, breaking off in the unfettered winds and bounding over the plains like tumbleweed, which incidentally is also edible when gathered very young and simmered until tender. The roots, thus, are left unmarked. To find them, the Indians had to harvest them

PRAIRIE TURNIP

in the early summer. They were then peeled and hung up in long strings to dry for winter use.

Prairie turnips, edible peeled and raw, were even better liked by the early settlers when boiled or roasted in small lone campfires. They can also be enjoyed in cakes. If you'd like to try some of these, wash, peel, and slice your wild tubers. You'll need about a pound to serve four. Simmer them, covered in a small amount of salted water until a fork will penetrate the largest of the pieces easily. Then drain and mash.

For every cup of mashed prairie turnips, mix in a tablespoon of butter or margarine. Whip together a teaspoon of flour, 1/2 teaspoon salt, 1/8 teaspoon pepper, and an egg yolk. Mix this with the prairie turnips. Mold into small, flat cakes, press into dry white bread crumbs, and sauté in a liberal amount of butter or margarine, turning them so as to brown them evenly.

Sometime when you want to serve four with a soup with a tantalizing flavor, simmer 1/2 pound of peeled and sliced prairie turnips in a minimum of salted water with a large sliced carrot and a large diced onion until everything is soft. Then drain and either strain or reduce to a pulp in a blender.

Put this pulp in a pan with a quart of milk, a tablespoon of butter or margarine, and salt and pepper to taste. Bring to a simmer, strew with a tablespoon of chopped water cress, and serve with thin, hot, buttered toast. If you'd really like to add a bit of tang and zip to the taste, allow 1/2 stick of butter or margarine to soften at room temperature and then mix 2 or 3 drops of tabasco with it. Spread the hot toast lightly with this.

THE COAST-TO-COAST DELICACY THAT GAVE A CITY ITS NAME

WILD ONION

(Allium)

WILD ONIONS, INCLUDING THE LEEKS, THE chives, and the garlics, grow wild all over North America except in the far northern regions. Indians used them extensively, not only for the provocative taste they impart to blander foods, but also as a main part of the meal. Settlers and frontiersmen soon followed suit.

When Père Marquette and his band journeyed from Green Bay, Wisconsin in 1674 to near our present Chicago—whose name is taken from the Indian word "shikato," meaning place where wild onions are strong-smelling—their main food was wild leeks, probably *Allium tricoccum,* whose flat leaves, some one to three inches broad, nod in the breezes from the Maritime Provinces to Iowa and Minnesota, south to the Carolinas.

For the most part, though, the wild onions have slender, quill-like leaves, similar to those of domestic varieties. They grow from bulbs. Flowers appear on otherwise naked shafts, arising like the ribs of an umbrella. The one characteristic on which to depend is the characteristic odor.

Although you probably won't like all the breed—especially not the strong-tasting field garlic, *Allium vineale,* which is an immigrant from Europe and which is beloved by cows in the East to the detriment of milk, cream, and butter—wild onions are all good to eat. The best way to find out your likes and dislikes is by trying them. Often you can use the entire plant.

However, have nothing whatsoever to do with any plants, wild or otherwise, that resemble the onion but do not have its familiar odor! Some bulbs whose appearance is superficially like that of onions are among the most concentrated of poisons. Your nose will be your own best protection.

By the way, it has been found that the odors that sometimes linger on the breath after one has eaten onions, chives, leeks, and garlic are entirely the result of solid particles remaining in the mouth. Brushing the teeth and tongue and rinsing the mouth after eating will do away with any fear of offending.

Wild onions simmered until tender in a small amount of lightly salted water, then drained and topped with butter or margarine or, for a change, mayonnaise, are fine fare. Save the liquid for soup or for other cooking.

If you want to go to a little more trouble, glazed wild onions are succulent. Simmer, covered, until they are nearly tender enough wild onions for four in a cup of either broth or water in which a chicken bouillon cube has been dissolved. Then drain off all but 3 tablespoons of the liquid. Add 1/2 stick of butter or margarine and 2 tablespoons of sugar. Simmer, uncovered now, for 20 minutes, basting and stirring gently every 5 minutes.

The Indians ate grouse, duck, quail, plover, and other wild eggs whenever possible, often cooking them with wild onions. Eggs and this wild vegetable still really go together. If you like fried eggs and have the time to impress some friends, try this recipe.

Blend thoroughly 2 tablespoons salad oil, 2 teaspoons lemon juice, 1/4 teaspoon salt, and a slight darkening of pepper.

WILD ONION

Cook a tablespoon of grated wild onion in this over low heat for 2 or 3 minutes. Then add a tablespoon of hot water and bring up the heat a bit. As soon as the liquid steams, slip 8 shelled eggs carefully from a dish into the frypan, cover, lower the heat again, and cook briefly until the whites are set. The results are so far from the tough, leathery objects so often served as "fried eggs" that you have to eat them to believe them.

When you don't want to go to that much trouble, why not scramble your eggs and wild onion. There's a trick to this, too, that you may care to adopt as your own. First, let the eggs come to room temperature. Then break 8 eggs into a bowl, add a tablespoon of cool water for each egg, and mix with a fork until well blended but not frothy. Add a teaspoon of chopped wild onion.

Melt 2 tablespoons of butter or margarine in a frypan just hot enough to sizzle a drop of water. Tip in the egg mixture and reduce the heat to low. When the eggs have started to harden, begin stirring them constantly with a fork. Remove them while they are still creamy and soft. Season to taste with pepper and salt. Serve at once on hot plates.

Then there's wild onion pie. Starting with a cold frypan, slowly cook 4 diced slices of bacon until the bits begin to color. Then melt 1/2 stick of butter or margarine around them. Sauté 3 cups of thinly sliced wild onions in this until they are golden. Then set off the heat. After they have cooled, mix them with 4 eggs that have been beaten with 1/4 cup of evaporated milk. Pour into an uncooked, 9-inch pastry shell, the recipe for wild grape pie being an apt one. Bake in a preheated moderate 350-degree oven about 45 minutes or until the crust is flaky and the contents set and temptingly tan. Eat while still steaming.

As the Indian nations knew well, wild onions will enhance the flavor of almost any game or wild vegetable. An odorous sauce that will really touch up the somewhat bland flavor of pheasant breasts, when the hunter of the house comes home with limits and you are assigning the rest of the bird to the soup kettle, is started by gently sautéing 1/2 cup of chopped wild onions in 3 tablespoons of butter or margarine until the still uncolored bits are just tender.

Then blend in 1 1/2 teaspoons flour, stirring all the time. Add 2 cups of sour cream and a tablespoon of lemon juice. Salt and pepper to taste. Bring to a bubble and, giving it an occasional stir, cook over low heat for 10 minutes. Strew with a tablespoon of chopped parsley, sprinkle with paprika, and cascade over the bronzed white meat.

For hot weather you can make a delicate chilled soup with wild onions. Using a deep saucepan, sauté until no more than a very light tan a cup of thinly sliced wild onions in 1/4 stick of butter or margarine. Then add 4 equally thinly sliced, medium-size potatoes and a cup of water. Simmer until everything is very tender. Drain, saving the liquid, and put the vegetables through a strainer or the blender.

Slowly cook 2 tablespoons of flour and 2 tablespoons of butter or margarine over very low heat, stirring until golden. Then pour in the fluid from the vegetables and 3 cups of rich milk. Bring to a simmer, add the vegetables, season to taste with salt and pepper, and allow to bubble for 5 minutes. Remove from the heat. Allow to cool and then chill in the refrigerator. Serve garnished with a tablespoon of chopped water cress and if possible with one of chopped wild chives.

Then there is a robust soup to make on cool fall days when you have plenty of odds and ends of venison with which to brew a sturdy, forthright stock. Moose is a favorite, but beef will do. You'll need 5 cups of stock for a wild onion soup to serve four.

Sauté 2 cups of sliced wild onions in a stick of butter or margarine, stirring until they are well browned. Then transfer them to a saucepan containing the stock, seasoned to taste with salt and pepper, 1/8 teaspoon mace, and a bay leaf. Simmer very gently for 15 minutes, removing the bay leaf after 5 minutes.

Then set 4 slices of toasted sourdough or other substantial white bread in a large casserole. Pour the soup over it and sprinkle with 1/2 cup of freshly grated Parmesan cheese. Place the casserole either in a preheated hot 425-degree oven or under the broiler. Heat until the cheese is melted and golden.

For a superb one-dish meal for four that can be stirred together in minutes, first sauté 1/2 cup of chopped wild onions until limp in 3 tablespoons of butter or margarine. Before the onions brown, add the contents of a large can of tomatoes, 1/8 teaspoon each of tarragon and basil, and a minced clove of garlic. Cook until bubbling throughout. Then add 9 eggs and stir continuously and slowly to scramble. Serve while everything is seething.

Or simmer your wild onions for four in a small amount of salted water until, still whole, they are just tender. Then arrange them in a greased casserole. In the meantime, be preparing a sauce by melting 3 tablespoons of butter or margarine in a saucepan over moderate heat, then smoothly stirring in 3 tablespoons of flour. Still stirring, pour in a cup of hot milk. All this will thicken when it comes to a bubble. Season to taste with pepper and salt. Now pour this over the onions, sprinkle liberally with white bread crumbs, and place in a moderate 350-degree oven for a half-hour or until browned.

THE BERRY THAT INDIANS RELISHED WITH BUFFALO

BUFFALO BERRY

(Shepherdia)

THE THREE VARIETIES OF BUFFALO BERRY native to the continental United States are the only species of the sort in the world. One or more of them flourishes in nearly every part of the country except the Southeast, including Alaska, making them prime emergency foods.

Black bears eat the fruit, and so do quail and flocks of other birds. Indians used to devour tremendous amounts of the berries, gathering them by the bushel. They used them as we do the currants they resemble, often making a pudding of them and the flour of the prairie turnip, described elsewhere in this book. Vast quantities, dried for winter use, were cooked with buffalo meat; hence the name.

Shepherdia canadensis is the type of buffalo berry with which many are most acquainted. Growing from Alaska and British Columbia to Newfoundland, south to the northern states and along the Rockies, this is a shrub some three to five feet tall. It prefers dry, well-drained habitats. The young buds and twigs are rough with reddish brown scales. The oval leaves, growing opposite to one another, are up to about two and one-half inches long and have smooth margins. Green above, beneath they are silvery or rusty with scales and dense hair. Small yellow flowers appear at the same time, growing in the angle between leaf and branch. The berries are small, round, translucent, and either a striking orange or scarlet.

The presence of saponin, found in many plants and used commercially as a foam producer, makes these berries a little too bitter ordinarily to be enjoyed raw in any quantity, although they are good when sweetened by frost and then dried with sugar. Indians, however, consider them great delicacies at any time. Their *modus operandi,* even today, is to mix the fruit with a little sugar, then beat it until it foams into a salmon-colored mass. Both tasty and nutritious, this is enjoyed on desserts as we use whipped cream.

BUFFALO BERRY

USE THIS FOR VITAMIN-TEEMING SALADS, PIES, AND SOUPS

LETTUCE SAXIFRAGE

(Saxifraga) (Micranthes)

THE "SAXIFRAGE" PART OF THE NAME comes from the Latin word meaning rock-breaker, a redoubtable and amusing designation for such a fragile little edible. Because it sometimes grows in rock fissures, the supposition arose that it split the stones. The lettuce saxifrage also abounds in moist meadows, along the cool edges of brooks, in marshy places, and on damp slopes from Pennsylvania on through the Appalachians to Tennessee. Edible cousins prosper over much of the country, except for the west central states, from Alaska and California to Georgia.

Also known as deer tongue because of the shape of its leaves and as mountain lettuce because of their edibility, lettuce saxifrage concentrates its growth in a crisp green rosette of leaves. The members of this thick mat are up to about eleven inches long, shaped like an animal's tongue and serrated with keen, short teeth.

When these leaves start to age and lose their tenderness, a flower stalk rises one or two feet from their midst, ending in a loosely branched cluster of small white flowers. These later develop sharply pointed, two-pronged seed capsules. In Alaska, with the *Saxifraga punctata,* this may be delayed until very late in the season in mountain and shoreline gulches where snow persists until midsummer.

The young, tender leaves, picked before the plant flowers, will supply considerable amounts of vitamins and flavor to salads. You may like them shredded with the fingers, tossed with 2 tablespoons of olive oil and the juice of 1/2 lemon, salted to taste, and garnished with sliced hard-cooked egg. Slices of cold lamb or chicken added to such a salad make a convenient and quickly prepared luncheon dish. Too, cold flaked fish is exceedingly nice mixed with it.

Wilted lettuce saxifrage is a favorite in numerous localities. Sauté 4 diced slices of bacon until crisp. Add 3 tablespoons cider vinegar, a tablespoon water, a teaspoon salt, and 1/8 teaspoon apiece of pepper and dry mustard. A little sour cream is also good. When everything is bubbling, tip in 4 cups of coarsely shredded young greens. Cook only until wilted. For a change on occasion, slice hot hard-cooked eggs over the top.

For lettuce saxifrage soup, a whiff of which will start the nostrils of a hungry man trembling, shred 4 cups of the young greens, again enough for four. Sauté a diced, medium-size onion in 2 tablespoons of butter or margarine until the bits are soft but not browned. Then stir in the greens, cover, and steam for 3 minutes. Add 3 cups of beef stock, made with bouillon cubes if necessary, and bring to a bubble for 10 minutes. Correct the seasoning. If you'd like something a bit more substantial, add 1 1/2 cups of cooked rice, a blend of the wild and the domestic being tasty. Serve steaming.

Finally, there is a vitamin-teeming lettuce saxifrage pie, as stimulating to the tongue as to the gastric fluids. Bring a small amount of salted water to a boil. Toss in 4 cups of the young greens, 1/2 cup of water cress, and 1/4 cup of chopped

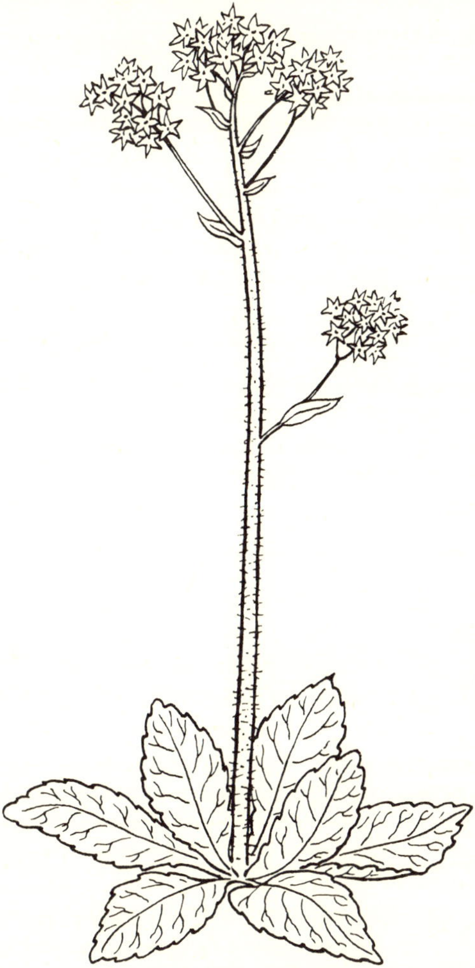

LETTUCE SAXIFRAGE

chives. Boil, covered, only until tender. Then drain, chop, and season to taste with salt, pepper, and a liberal amount of paprika.

Beat 3 eggs with a pint of half-and-half. Stir in 1/4 cup of flour until you have a smooth thin batter. Mix this well with the vegetables and pour into a casserole. Cook in a moderate 350-degree oven until an appetizing crust covers the top. Start 2 tablespoons of chipped butter or margarine melting over everything, sprinkle on more paprika, and serve.

A WILD GREEN YOU CAN GROW IN YOUR CELLAR

POKEWEED

(Phytolacca)

THE FIRST WILD GREENS OF THE spring in many a happy household, pokeweed flourishes in the eastern half of the country except along the Canadian border, west to Texas and south to the tropics. The Indians found it delicious, and some of the first European adventurers on these shores were in such agreement that they took the seeds back to France and southern Europe, where the vegetable became popular. Today pokeweed finds its way into many of our stores as a springtime delicacy. Some devotees like it so well that they even grow it in their cellars.

Also known as pokeberry, poke, scoke, pigeonberry, garget, coakum, and inkberry, this wild vegetable has a huge perennial root often as large as a man's forearm. Fibrous and covered with a thin tannish bark, this can be easily broken to size and planted in garden soil in a deep, flat box. Best are the medium-size roots, some three or four inches in diameter, broken or cut into six-inch lengths, dug and replanted indoors after the first heavy freeze of fall. Kept in a dark, warm cellar and regularly watered, these will regularly send up shoots for months. For a family of three, you'll want about a dozen such roots.

The fat young sprouts, especially when they are some six to eight inches high, are the only part of pokeweed that is good to eat. The bitter roots—cathartic, emetic, and somewhat narcotic—are poisonous. So are the mature stalks when they take on a purplish cast. You may have seen birds get tipsy on the berries.

You'll want to be able to recognize the full-grown plants, however, as in the spring it is near their dried remains that the tender young shoots will arrow upward. These annuals grow into round stalks, about an inch in diameter, which reach and branch upwards from four to nine feet. The leaves, which are shaped like rounded lances, have stems on one end and points on the other. Scattered, smooth on both sides, and wavy-margined, they are up to about ten inches long.

Both flowers and fruit grow in long clusters on short stems. The numerous, small flowers are a greenish white. The round, ripe berries are a deep purple and are an important source of food for the mourning dove. Their reddish purple juice, as boys sometimes used to confirm in the fall when school classes were first resuming, will serve as an ink for steel pen points.

Gather your small, tender pokeweed shoots when they are no more than about eight inches tall. Remove skin and leaves, saving the latter for greens. Simmer the whole stems in a small amount of lightly salted water for 10 minutes or until tender. Serve on hot buttered toast, steaming with sauce.

One sauce whose flavor really brings out the springlike deliciousness of young pokeweed is started by finely chopping 2 slices of a medium-size onion, then tanning the bits in 2 tablespoons of butter or margarine. Then blend in 3 tablespoons flour. Slowly add a cup of milk, stirring vigorously. Mix in a teaspoon of chopped water cress. Salt and pepper to taste, sprinkle with 1/8 teaspoon nutmeg, and simmer gently

POKEWEED

for 5 minutes, stirring occasionally. Add 1/4 cup of heavy cream, bring again to a bubble, and serve.

A tantalizing cheese sauce to touch up the flavor of such pokeweed on toast can be made by slowly melting 2 tablespoons of butter or margarine in a saucepan over moderate heat, not allowing it to brown. Then smoothly stir in an equal volume of flour. Stirring vigorously, gradually add 1 1/4 cups of milk and bring to a bubble. Season with 1/4 teaspoon salt and 1/8 teaspoon pepper. Still stirring, simmer for 5 minutes to take away the raw taste of the flour. Now remove from the heat for several minutes. Add a bit at a time, stirring energetically until each portion has melted before adding more, 3/4 cup of good grated American cheese. Return to low heat but do not allow to boil. Spoon over each serving, dust with paprika and with parsley flakes, and see what everyone's idea is for vegetables the next day.

Pokeweed is also good with eggs. For this dish, skin the shoots but leave on the little unfurled leaves at the top. Wash well. Then boil whole for 8 minutes in salted water until nearly tender. Drain, saving 1/4 cup of the fluid. Mix this liquid with 3 beaten eggs, 3 tablespoons salad oil, a halved clove of garlic, and salt and pepper to taste. Add to the pokeweed and, stirring occasionally, cook about 2 minutes or until the latter is ready for the table. Remove the garlic and serve.

For a rich, aromatic soup, simmer 2 cups of pokeweed shoots until soft and then put either through a sieve or the blender. Bring 2 cups of milk to a bubble along with a halved clove of garlic. Then discard the garlic and add the pureed vegetable. Mix 3 tablespoons flour smoothly with a small amount of cold water. Stir that, along with 3 tablespoons of butter or margarine, into the soup. Season to taste with salt and pepper. Bring again to a bubble, add a tablespoon of chopped water cress and a cup of heavy cream, sprinkle with paprika, and serve steaming.

Those times when bachelors are doing the cooking they sometimes go in a lot for one-dish meals, and this wild vegetable is one of those lending itself well to such production. Simmer until tender in a minimum amount of salted water enough young pokeweed for four. In the meantime, be preparing a white sauce by melting 1/2 stick of butter or margarine in a saucepan, smoothly stirring in 1/4 cup flour, and then, still stirring, slowly adding 2 cups milk. Season to taste with salt and pepper. Stir in 2 tablespoons of finely diced green pepper. Bring to a simmer.

Also be simmering 4 eggs, completely covered with water, for 8 to 10 minutes depending on their size. Then remove them from the heat and plunge them into cold water. Crack the shells slightly before the eggs cool, so that peeling will be easier. Slice.

Spread a base of pokeweed over the bottom of a well-greased casserole. Cover with white sauce, then with sliced egg. Repeat until all the ingredients are used. Top with 1/2 cup of buttered white bread crumbs. Bake in a moderate 325-degree oven for half an hour. Serve hot. Just a whiff of this will have your customers waiting eagerly.

SEACOAST HARVEST THAT CAN PEP UP YOUR THYROID

DULSE

(Rhodymenia)

DULSE IS SO PROLIFIC ALONG OUR Atlantic and Pacific coasts that it grows from other seaweeds as well as from submerged rocks and ledges. Rich in vital minerals including iodine, the ingredient necessary for the proper functioning of the thyroid gland, this popular chewable is more popular in Europe than on this continent, although in places like New Brunswick you find it for sale in small grocery stores.

These sea plants have extremely brief stems that rapidly widen into thin, elastic fronds. Varying in color from purplish to reddish, these smooth flat expanses are frequently lobed and cleft. The whole seaweed grows from a few inches to about a foot in length.

The Indians in southeast Alaska still gather this seaweed in quantity, usually during the low tides of May and early June. They then dry it in the sun and air as they do laver, eventually storing it for adding during the winter to soups and stews. It is also used fresh. Chewed directly from the sea, it is tough and rubbery. The trick is to hang it or spread it out until it is partially dry. Or if you don't want to wait that long, just singe the fresh dulse on a hot stove, griddle, or campfire rock.

A premium you sometimes come by when harvesting dulse in Alaska during the midsummer herring runs is herring roe.

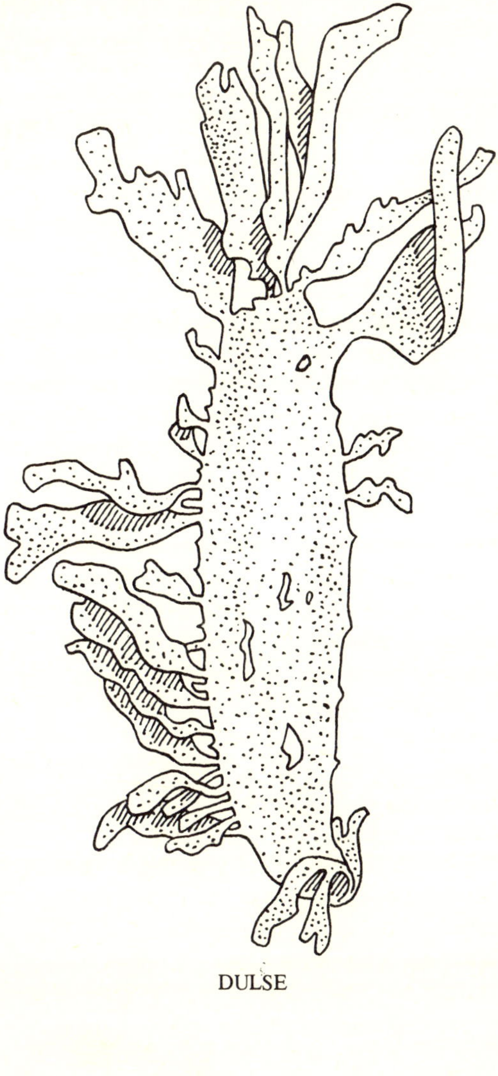

DULSE

All you have to do is drain this roe, season it with pepper and salt, and sauté it in butter or margarine in moderate heat until brown on both sides. About 12 minutes will do the job. Then add lemon juice to butter or margarine that's been heated to a delicate brown and pour this over the hot roe. Enjoy at once.

This dulse-enmeshed herring roe is also scrambled with eggs in Alaska. For about 1/2 pound of roe, add a tablespoon of vinegar and another of salt to 2 cups of boiling water. Put in the roe and simmer it for 15 minutes before draining it and removing the membrane. Then mash. Combine with 6 eggs, 6 tablespoons cream, 1/2 teaspoon salt, and 1/8 teaspoon pepper. Scramble in 2 tablespoons butter or margarine in a frypan over low heat. Garnish with chopped dried dulse and serve hot.

As for the dulse itself, it can be used to add character to such dishes as otherwise rather tasteless tuna loaf. Mix 2 cups of flaked or grated cooked tuna with 1/2 cup of the chopped soft fronds of dried dulse. Add 1/2 cup of soft bread crumbs, 1/2 stick butter or margarine, 2 well-beaten eggs, a tablespoon apiece of chopped onion and water cress, and pepper and Worcestershire to taste. Turn into a buttered baking dish and bake in a preheated 375-degree oven until firm. This is excellent hot, swimming in a sauce made by heating a cup of white sauce with 1/4 cup each of mayonnaise and chopped stuffed olives.

THE PICK OF THE EDIBLE WILD GREENS

ORACH

(Atriplex)

IN A LOT OF HOMES ACROSS the continent the acknowledged pick of the edible greens is orach. The tender tips and juicy young leaves of this wild edible are delicious from spring to late fall. Connoisseurs pronounce them equal to, if not better than, the green amaranth, to which the plant bears some resemblance.

Orach provides top eating from British Columbia to Labrador, south to California and Virginia, growing luxuriantly on salt marshes and wet flats along the coasts and on moist alkaline lands in the interior. Shaped somewhat like lance heads, the leaves are grayish to bright green, smooth-edged, and characteristically lighter and mealy-looking underneath. The small, green flowers grow in narrow spikelike clusters. Later there is an abundance of small, starchy seeds, once ground by some of the Indian tribes for meal.

Also known as saltbush and as shad scale, orach is a favorite food of the big Canada goose, which feeds on its seeds, leaves, and stems. Quail are among the upland game birds dining on the seeds. Deer, rabbits, antelopes, mountain sheep, and some of the remaining herds of bison browse on the twigs and foliage.

You have to be careful not to add too much salt to orach, but outside of that it can be used in any of the recipes in this book for wild greens. Too, there are these particularly efficacious dishes.

Few green salads are as tasty as those made with young orach, washed, dried, and, if you're not going to use it right away, wrapped in a towel to stay crisp in the refrigerator. For something a little different, mix orach with sliced apples, slivers of peeled lemon, a few broken walnut meats, and a generous sprinkling of grated Cheddar cheese. A dressing that will really bring out the flavor of all this is made by mixing and chilling 1/2 cup olive oil, 3 tablespoons lemon juice, a tablespoon of finely chopped pickles, 1/2 teaspoon finely minced chives, 1/2 teaspoon chopped parsley, 1/4 teaspoon paprika, 1/8 teaspoon pepper, and salt to taste.

Orach brings out the savor of fruit, and you may like to blend it in a salad bowl with such availables as thin slices of orange, pear, apples, and slivers of banana touched up with lemon juice. Dress this salad liberally with mayonnaise and paprika just before serving.

For a wilted salad of tender young orach, wash and dry 4 cups of the greens. Place them in a salad bowl that has been well rubbed with a later discarded halved clove of garlic. Brown 4 diced slices of bacon over low heat in a frypan. When it is crisp, turn off the heat and quickly stir in 1/4 cup of wine vinegar, a teaspoon of chopped chives, and 1/8 teaspoon pepper. As soon as everything is steaming, pour over the orach, cover, and let stand 5 minutes. Then toss again, using a spoon and fork gently as always so as not to bruise the leaves, and serve.

Young orach cooks up quickly. Just wash it well, then put it into a saucepan without added water and cook it, tightly covered, until barely tender. Serve hot with pepper, a little salt if yoũ want, and a scattering of lemon juice.

ORACH

Baked orach provides an artful change of pace. Toss 4 cups of the greens in 1/2 stick of butter or margarine over low heat in a frypan until everything is well mixed. Then put in a casserole and pepper and salt to taste, being careful not to add too much of the latter. Mix 1/2 cup of dried white bread crumbs with a cup of cream and pour over the top. Sprinkle with grated Parmesan cheese, touch up with paprika and a suggestion of parsley flakes, and bake in a moderate 350-degree oven until very hot.

For a cream soup with a delicate warmth of color, aroma, and taste, you'll need a cup of cooked, chopped orach. Mix this in the blender with 3 cups of milk, or if you want something really luxurious, cream. Add 3 tablespoons butter, 1 tablespoon flour, 1/4 teaspoon dry mustard, and 1/8 teaspoon pepper. Blend until everything is smooth. Then tip into a saucepan and bring to a simmer, salting to taste and stirring until the soup is somewhat thick and has a full-bodied savor.

Another particularly tasty soup for four is started by slowly heating a cup of chopped orach and 1/2 cup of chopped water cress in 2 tablespoons of butter or margarine for 5 minutes. Then add 4 cups of some broth, made with bouillon cubes if necessary. Cover and simmer 10 minutes. Remove from the heat, stir in 1/2 cup of heavy cream that has been beaten with an egg yolk, check for salt, strew with pepper and with a little paprika for contrast, and ladle out.

Fritters, anyone? For four satisfied diners cook 4 cups of orach until tender, tightly covered, in the water that clings to them after rinsing. Then strain, chop, and place in a bowl. Stir in the yolks of 2 eggs, 1/2 cup freshly grated Parmesan cheese, a tablespoon of butter or margarine, and 1/4 teaspoon nutmeg. When the mixture has cooled to room temperature, beat the 2 egg whites and fold them in. Drop the batter by the tablespoon into very shallow hot fat and fry until golden all over. Drain on absorbent paper, and you're in business.

EXPENSIVE WILD SWEET THAT MAY GROW FREE ON YOUR STREET

MAPLE

(Acer)

THE MAPLE LEAF, EMBLEM OF CANADA and a principal reason why northern New England is so colorful in the autumn—especially when frost-hazed nights are succeeded by brisk, smoky days—is known to everyone. The fruits, too, are very characteristic, being made up of a pair of brown wings with the seeds enclosed in the plump juncture.

Maple seeds are edible by humans, some Indians formerly hulling the larger of them and then boiling them. So are the leaves. The inner bark of the maple is one of the more appetizing sap layers and is eaten in emergencies, either raw or cooked. But it is for the sap that the tree has been famous since Indian days.

Wild turkeys, quail, grouse, and prairie chickens eat maple buds, twigs, and seeds. Black bears, rabbits, beavers, and squirrels dine on flowers, seeds, bark, and twigs. Incidentally, before they store the seeds for winter use, squirrels often thriftily remove the hulls and wings. Deer, moose, elk, and mountain sheep relish twigs and foliage.

The first settlers to venture along the Atlantic seaboard were introduced to the wild sweet by the red men, who caught the sap in birchbark containers and in tightly woven baskets and skin vessels. All the maples have sugar-rich sap. So do other trees, for that matter, such as the birch and hickory. But it is the sugar maple, *Acer saccharum*, that is by far the most famous for this characteristic. Incidentally, the tree is perhaps the most prized of the hardwoods in the lumber industry. It is also a highly desirable shade and ornamental tree, so perhaps you have your own private source of maple sugar growing right by your own home.

Groves of maple trees, with the rude sugar houses, are familiar landmarks in many parts of the country, inasmuch as the sugar maple grows from Newfoundland to Ontario and Minnesota, southward as far as Louisiana and Georgia. The trees, often reaching a height of from sixty to almost a hundred feet, are tapped in late winter or early spring, before the buds begin to expand. Sharp frosty nights, followed by mild thawing during the daylight hours, make for the free flow of sap. The sweetness of this varies, but it usually takes between thirty and forty gallons to boil down into a gallon of the high-priced syrup.

Additional boiling makes maple sugar. During early American years, this was about the consistency of present-day brown sugar. In fact, it was used in place of cane sugar by colonists who couldn't afford the then much more expensive sweetening, even when it was available. Maple sugar is still more nourishing than the mass manufactured product, containing the B vitamins, calcium, phosphorus, and enzymes refined from today's sugar beets and sugar cane.

You can buy the necessary spiles and pails for sap gathering. Unless you are going in for sugaring in a big way, though, you can do very well on your own. The Indians used to cut a "V"-shaped gash in the tree, at the apex of which they drove an elderberry spout. The latter was made by cutting straight elderberry limbs in the spring, drying them with the leaves on, and then poking out the soft pith of their interiors with hot sticks.

You may find it more conservative to drill about a two-inch-deep hole with a gimlet, or brace and bit, and to close this with a peg when you're finished. For the spout, just make a single bend in a can top cut off by one of the smooth-cutting openers. Don't try to suspend the pail from this, however. Instead, drive a nail into the tree for this purpose. As a precaution, empty the containers often enough so that the sap doesn't hang too long in the sun and sour.

Then it's just a matter of boiling the sap, and spooning off the characteristic scum as it rises, until some thirty-five or so parts of water evaporate, leaving a clear amber syrup. This you'll want to strain very carefully. Or, for sugar, you'll wish to continue boiling until a test portion of the syrup forms a very soft ball in cold water. Then remove from the fire, beat with an egg beater if you're making only a small amount or a regular sugar beater if you have a large quantity, and pour into dry molds.

One's first sugaring-off party is in the same category as that initial seashore clambake—unforgettable! I remember as a small boy riding out to a hillside maple bush behind two glistening horses in a pung. Syrup was already bubbling in the sugar house with an elusive and marvelous odor, and they gave me a small pitcher of it and an old fork.

Everything must have been ready, for when I strung this amber liquid out in a fine line on fresh snow, it hardened. Even before it was cool enough, I twined the string on my fork and transferred it gingerly to my mouth. This I repeated until all the syrup was gone, and then I got some more. The flavor was indescribable, except that there was the aroma of the forest in its sweetness—the fresh wind blowing, the branches swinging overhead, and all the free, rich wildness of the mountains themselves.

You'll get snow in your boots at a sugaring-off party and there'll be an occasional bit of bark in your sweet. But you won't give either a second thought. It's worth it a dozen times over.

The Indians used to blend their maple syrup and maize, and the marriage is still a happy one. For steaming chunks of maple corn bread, broken from a hot loaf, sift together a cup of all-purpose flour, a cup of cornmeal, 4 teaspoons baking powder, and a teaspoon salt. Stir together 2 beaten eggs, 1/2 cup melted shortening, and 1/3 cup maple syrup. Now blend the two mixtures as thoroughly and quickly as possible. Pour without delay into a greased pan and bake in a preheated very hot 450-degree oven for about 20 minutes or until a straw inserted in the loaf comes out clean.

Or maybe you'd like some maple muffins. Beat an egg with 1/4 cup of milk. Sift together 1 3/4 cups of all-purpose flour, 3 teaspoons of baking powder, and 1/4 teaspoon of salt. Stir into the milk mixture, along with 1/2 cup of maple syrup, a bit at a time. Then fold in 1/2 stick melted butter or margarine. Bake in a warmed, greased muffin pan in a preheated moderate 350-degree oven for about 20 minutes or until done.

Maple buns are another possibility. Sift together 2 cups all-purpose flour, 3 teaspoons baking powder, and 1 teaspoon salt. Cut in 1/2 cup of shortening until everything has the texture of rough cornmeal. Then, taking a fork, stir the mixture gently but quickly into a soft dough with about 2/3 cup milk. Have a muffin pan well greased and each container holding a tablespoon of maple syrup, a scant tablespoon of slivered almonds, and 1/8 teaspoon melted butter or margarine.

Fill each 3/4 full of dough. Put at once into a preheated hot 425-degree oven and bake about 15 minutes or until golden.

For about 2 dozen maple rolls, sift together 2 1/2 cups all-purpose flour, 1/4 cup baking powder, and a teaspoon of

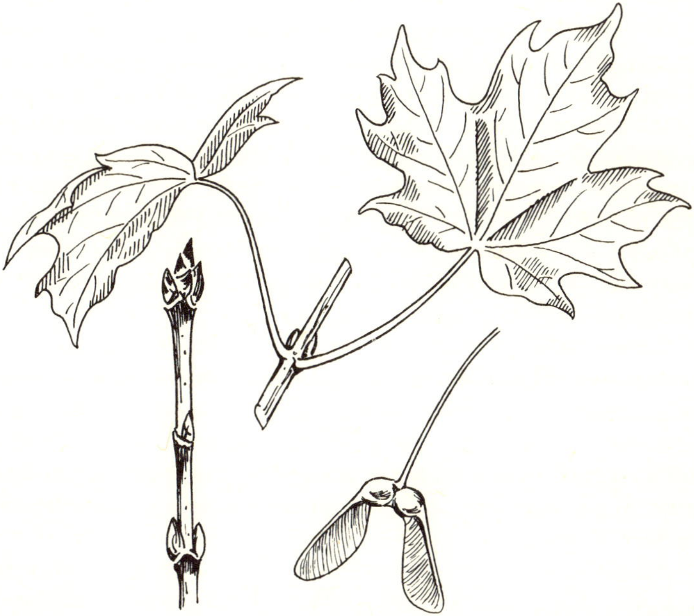

MAPLE

salt. Cut in 1/2 stick of butter or margarine until the mixture is the consistency of cornmeal. Beat an egg and a cup of milk and blend. Knead very briefly, then roll out into a 1/4-inch-thick rectangle. Brush with melted butter or margarine and dust with finely crumbled maple sugar. Roll, cut into 1-inch slices, place apart in a greased baking pan, brush again with melted butter or margarine, and bake in a preheated very hot 450-degree oven for about 12 minutes or until golden brown.

Then there is the dessert based on biscuits. Sift together 2 cups all-purpose flour, 2 teaspoons baking powder, 1/2 teaspoon salt, and 1/4 teaspoon cream of tartar. Cut in 1/4 cup shortening. Add enough milk, about 1/2 cup, to make a soft dough. Roll this out about 1/2-inch thick and cut a dozen small biscuits. Place these in a shallow greased pan and top each with several chips of butter or margarine and a slight dusting of cinnamon. Have a cup of maple syrup bubbling on top of the stove. Pour this now over the biscuits. Place at once in a preheated hot 425-degree oven and bake 15 minutes or until done. Serve hot with either whipped cream or with scoops of butter pecan ice cream.

Occasions when you're not hungry enough for any of the above, appetite-stimulating maple toast smells almost as good as it tastes. You can use a toaster if it browns one side of the bread at a time. After the first side is tanned, butter the second, strew it with soft maple sugar, dust with cinnamon, and return it to the heat until the sugar has melted. Otherwise, use the oven.

For a maple sauce with which to top squash, apple, pumpkin, and blueberry desserts, whip a cup of heavy cream into soft peaks. Then tip 1/4 cup of maple syrup across the top and carefully fold it in. Season with a scattering of grated nutmeg.

Another maple sauce, one many especially like when it is spreading over hot cereal, is made by crumbling 1/2 pound of maple sugar, stirring in 3 tablespoons boiling water, and heating at a bubble until all the sugar is dissolved. Add a sprinkle of nutmeg. Then remove from the stove and mix in a stick of butter or margarine.

Maple syrup and cream is always a felicitous combination. Boil a cup of heavy cream with a cup of maple syrup until a sample forms a very soft ball in cold water. Then whip with an eggbeater for 2 minutes. If you are going to use this atop vanilla ice cream, you may like to stir in 1/3 cup of chopped walnuts or pecans.

Or for a simple and delicately flavored candy, boil 2 cups of maple syrup, a cup of whipping cream, and 1/8 teaspoon of salt until a thread forms when a bit is dribbled off the tip of a spoon. Then cool and beat until dense and creamy. Drop the individual candies from a spoon onto waxed paper.

You can make enough frosting for, say, an 8-inch layer cake with either maple sugar or maple syrup. For the first, heat and stir 2 cups maple sugar and a cup of light cream until a test portion forms a soft ball in cold water. Remove from the stove, cool a bit, and then work with an eggbeater until creamy.

For the second, boil 2 cups of maple syrup without stirring until a test portion runs off the tip of a spoon in a long thread. Then pour gradually over 3 stiffly beaten egg whites. Beat until thick enough to apply with a knife. If you want, 1/2 cup of chopped nuts can be added during the last stage to either of these frostings. Walnuts, pecans, and toasted almonds are tasty. For a real taste thrill, though, try piñons.

For some memorable cookies, sift together 2 cups of all-purpose flour, 2 teaspoons baking powder, and 1/4 teaspoon salt. Cream a cup of finely crushed maple sugar with 1/2 cup of shortening. Beat an egg with 1/4 cup of milk. Now mix everything into a dough, ball this, either wrap in waxed paper or foil or place in a covered bowl, and leave in the refrigerator overnight.

The next day preheat the oven to a moderate 375 degrees. Roll the dough out very thin on a floured board, rectangle of plastic, or pastry cloth. Cut and bake on a sparingly greased cooky sheet for 8 to 10 minutes or until lightly browned. These will be dainty and crisp.

If you like ham, you owe it to yourself to bake at least one with maple syrup. First, try a slice an inch thick, parboiled to freshen it. Stud this with cloves and place in a casserole. Mix a cup of maple syrup with 2 tablespoons cider vinegar and 2 teaspoons dry mustard. Pour this over the meat and bake in a moderate 375-degree oven for 45 minutes, occasionally basting with the sauce. Delectable!